A GUIDE TO MEDIATING IN SCOTLAND

A GUIDE TO MEDIATING IN SCOTLAND

Edited by

EWAN A MALCOM and FIONA B O'DONNELL

DUNDEE UNIVERSITY PRESS
2009

First published in Great Britain in 2009 by
Dundee University Press
University of Dundee
Dundee DD1 4HN

www.dup.dundee.ac.uk

ISBN 978-1-84586-052-3

No natural forests were destroyed to make this product;
only farmed timber was used and replanted.

British Library Cataloguing-in-Publication Data
A catalogue for this book is available on request from the British Library.

Typeset by Waverley Typesetters, Fakenham
Printed and bound by Bell & Bain Ltd, Glasgow

CONTENTS

PREFACE

I welcome this compendious review of mediation in Scotland. Ewan Malcolm is Director and Fiona O'Donnell is a board member of the Scottish Mediation Network which has contributed so much to the growth and success of mediation in Scotland in recent years.

In 2003 I was a member of a delegation led by the Scottish Consumer Council which studied the highly developed system of mediation in Maryland. That visit persuaded me of the value of mediation, not only as a means of diverting disputes from the courts but as a means of promoting amity in the resolution of them.

This Guide will be valued by all who take part in mediation and will stimulate discussion of the important questions that it raises. I hope that it will lead to the development of a Scottish literature of mediation.

The Right Honourable Lord Gill, Lord Justice Clerk of Scotland

INTRODUCTION

Co-operating for mutual benefit — collaboration — is at the heart of how mediation works.

In our relatively small and awesomely beautiful corner of north-west Europe, mediators have been engaged in the heavy lifting of long-term and sustained co-operation. From community to commercial and from additional support needs to workplace, conflict management experts have found a common cause. They unite around the shared vision that mediation will become embedded into the culture of Scotland.

Mediation is seldom the easy option. It requires people to persevere in a respectful manner rather than squaring up to the fight or throwing in the towel. Mediators encourage them to retain responsibility for resolving the conflict which is, often, causing them considerable grief. In remarkably complex situations, mediators stick with it tenaciously.

The task of bringing together a diverse and, sometimes, competing assembly of interests is equally hard. It takes willingness, it takes focus and it needs a supportive environment. Over the last six years the Scottish Mediation Network has fulfilled this function. It has allowed the growth of unexpected innovation. Creative originality is possible every day in our field of work and this book is a shining example.

The contributors to this book, comprising, in the main, members of the Board of the Scottish Mediation Network, the Standards Board of the Scottish Mediation Register and the SMN staff team, have provided the rich material contained in each chapter. Their enthusiastic willingness to participate in this project as volunteers has turned our job into a real pleasure.

We launched this project in July 2007, so by April 2008 we were very grateful to Dr Ian Francis (Academic Secretary and Director of

Academic Affairs, University of Dundee) for his direct and encouraging comments on the draft chapters and to Karen Smith for her time and assistance in bringing together first draft comments.

We owe a great debt of gratitude to Toni Freitas (responsible for Publications and Events at the Scottish Mediation Network) who applied her considerable literary skills to proofreading and content editing the book as it was drawn together as a comprehensive whole. We are also grateful to the Scottish Government Justice Ministers and their officials, especially Lorna Gibbon, for their support and funding.

This book was first suggested by the University Secretary, Dr David Duncan. Carole Dalgleish and Carol Pope at Dundee University Press have been unfailingly helpful.

We hope that the reader finds what he or she needs in this book. We aim for it to be clear, succinct and useful. More information can be found at www.scottishmediation.org.uk.

Each chapter has a different voice and offers an insight into the different areas of mediation in Scotland. We expect that readers will use this book either to get an overview of mediation working across various spheres or to dip into the particular areas of interest covered by each chapter, with signposting to further information.

EWAN A MALCOLM and FIONA B O'DONNELL
11 December 2008

ENDORSEMENTS

In the half-dozen years when I've been privileged to be Patron of the Scottish Mediation Network I've had the opportunity to meet and learn from mediators from a wide variety of backgrounds and cultures. Everything I've seen and heard confirms the view that mediation has a crucial and healing role to play across the whole spectrum of human activity.

Formal and informal, politically high powered or community based, within or separate from the judicial process, mediation has enjoyed an ever higher profile and attracted a huge amount of respect, often from former sceptics.

My own journey of observation has taken me from initial agnosticism to full-blown evangelist. I'm sure the experience and commitment which shines through this publication can only enhance the reputation of Scottish mediation and give further encouragement to present and future practitioners.

Ruth Wishart, writer and broadcaster

Many congratulations to the Scottish mediation community, most notably Ewan Malcolm and Fiona O'Donnell, on this most impressive accomplishment.

Your *Guide to Mediating in Scotland* does not simply celebrate the achieve-ment of a milestone, it acknowledges and values the process and even the very arduousness of doing so. The ideas and expertise contained in this impressive volume define and reflect the ultimate goal — to create a more peaceful and civil society — and deign to suggest a means for accomplishing that goal. In addition, the Guide, rather than contenting itself to chronicle some of the tremendous progress made in recent years to advance the Scottish use of mediation, contributes to the ongoing global discourse about mediation excellence.

We, the Maryland Judiciary, have benefited greatly from a fruitful and collaborative relationship with the Scottish Mediation Network. We, working through our Mediation and Conflict Resolution Office, and the Network have learned much from each other over the past five years, as each has pursued the shared goal, in the process, making progress in its efforts to reform the courts into more efficient and user-friendly institutions and to foster a new culture of conflict resolution.

I am honored to have played a small part in your efforts. I look forward to our continued work together.

The Honorable Robert M Bell,
Chief Judge of the Maryland Court of Appeals

Conflicts come in all sizes, shapes, colors and textures. One of the great challenges of our time is to re-capture the missed opportunities and lost time and money that occur when unnecessary disputes are prolonged.

Ewan Malcolm, Fiona O'Donnell, and the authors of *A Guide to Mediating in Scotland* have done a great service to the country. They have gathered together in one place everything that mediation users and practitioners might need by way of a reference and guide. Read it. Use it. And pass the knowledge on to others.

Peter Adler, PhD, President and CEO of The Keystone Center
and author of Eye-of-the-Storm Leadership

Competence at the mediation table is the key to fair agreements, satisfied parties and successful peacemaking careers. *A Guide to Mediating in Scotland* is a contribution to increasing mediator competence not only in Scotland but around the world. Each chapter is written by a veteran practitioner, so that the book is both practical and the authors' recommendations have credibility due to their experience in the field. In one volume that is easy to navigate, readers can gain an overview of the mediation process and more detailed strategies and tips for specialised areas of practice. I am proud to offer this book as a resource to participants in my mediation training courses and it is in my office's Client Library for clients to prepare for their own mediations.

Forrest S Mosten, author of Mediation Career Guide
(Jossey-Bass, 2001) and Collaborative Divorce Handbook
(forthcoming from Jossey-Bass in 2009)

AUTHOR BIOGRAPHIES

Deirdre Armstrong, MA (Hons), MSc undertook mediation training in 2006, following over 20 years as a business executive and management facilitator. She has worked in both private and public sectors, including being Scottish Managing Director of an international auction house and Management Development Advisor to the Scottish Health Service. She is an experienced, independent Scottish Mediation registered mediator. In addition to her mediation interests she is a regional representative of The Art Fund, the UK's leading art charity. She lives with her family in Edinburgh.

Rosanne Cubitt is a family mediator with the Relationships Scotland South Lanarkshire Family Mediation Service, and she is also trained in child consultation. Rosanne is currently Head of Professional Practice at Relationships Scotland, with responsibility for ensuring that family mediation practitioners who work for the network of local family mediation services are fully supported. This involves leading the development of foundation training and a continuous professional development programme, as well as ensuring that practice standards and policies are maintained. Rosanne has also been involved in the development of new services such as homelessness or intergenerational mediation, and parenting after separation groups.

Carol Hope has worked in the field of family mediation since 1991. She is a practising family mediator and supervisor and provides training and consultancy to mediation service providers. Carol works for the Scottish Mediation Network, developing Peer Mediation in schools. Carol works with organisations in conflict and is a practising workplace mediator. She also works as a sessional mediator for ASN mediation provider Common Ground Mediation. Carol has experience of working with children and young people with additional support needs on a one-to-one basis, to help improve communication and social skills. In addition, Carol works as a sessional disability conciliator with the Disability Conciliation Service.

Ewan A Malcolm, WS, LLB, Dip LP, NP set up the Scottish Mediation Network office in September 2002 and was appointed as its first Director. Ewan was in private practice as a lawyer for nearly two decades and started his mediation training in 1995. He practises as a commercial, family and community mediator, freelancing as a mediator in high-value family and commercial disputes. He is Director of Training for CALM, the association of family law mediators accredited by the Law Society of Scotland. He sits on the Policy Group of Lord Gill's Civil Courts Review. Ewan also volunteers with both the Edinburgh Sheriff Court and the Edinburgh Community Mediation Services, where he has completed the SVQ Level IV qualification in mediation. At the Law Awards of Scotland 2008, Ewan was named their first ever Mediator of the Year.

Marjorie Mantle is an experienced court, commercial and workplace mediator and managed the Edinburgh Sheriff Court Mediation Service for three and a half years until July 2008. Marjorie was responsible for setting up and running the mediation section of the Scottish Legal Complaints Commission which started in October 2008. In 2007 she started Mediation Scotland LLP and the following year was appointed Honorary Lecturer at the School of Law, University of Dundee. Since completing her law degree in 1982, Marjorie has undertaken commercial work for private- and public-sector organisations in Australia, New Zealand, the USA, Europe, England and Scotland.

Ian McDonough is SACRO's Mediation Advisor. Ian manages its Scottish Community Mediation Centre (SCMC), which assists local authorities in planning and setting up mediation services. The SCMC also provides high-quality training and consultancy work in Community Mediation and constructive conflict resolution. Previously, Ian was Manager of Edinburgh Community Mediation. He is an experienced mediator and trainer and sits on the Board of Directors of the Scottish Mediation Network. He is a qualified Community Education worker and has run projects in the fields of citizens' rights, welfare rights and community advocacy.

John Moffat has been employed within the public sector in various departments and roles for over 20 years, including 10 years as a full-time trade union officer and over 10 years in HR-related posts. Currently heading conduct and behavioural services in the Scottish Prison Service, John is head of the internal mediation service and deals with policies in relation to equality, conduct, grievances and bullying. John is also active in workplace mediation networks across Scotland through the Scottish Mediation Network and within the public sector via a Civil Service Network. John is often involved in presentations and events promoting, developing and expanding the use of mediation in the workplace.

Fiona B O'Donnell currently works as the University Solicitor and Legal Counsellor at the University of Dundee. Fiona became interested in mediation in 2003. She has since tried to incorporate the principles of mediation in her work. This resulted in the establishment of a discrete early dispute resolution facility within the University in October 2007, which Fiona leads. She first trained with Core Mediation in 2004, and was accredited as a mediator by the Law Society of Scotland in 2005. In 2008 Fiona became a CEDR-accredited mediator and received a CEDR Special Commendation Award in the Innovation Category for her work in early dispute resolution in Higher Education. Fiona is presently a board member of the Scottish Mediation Network and a registered mediator on the Scottish Mediation Register.

Eileen Schott has worked for SACRO, the largest provider of mediation services in Scotland, since 1998. She started as a volunteer mediator and then became a full-time mediation worker with Edinburgh Community Mediation Service, dealing with neighbour disputes. Using her teaching and training qualifications, Eileen transferred to SACRO's Community Mediation Consultancy and Training Service in 2000 as a mediation trainer and assessor and is currently a Mediation Practice Specialist at the Scottish Community Mediation Centre and is also Chair of the Scottish Mediation Network Board.

Roger Sidaway previously worked in government before becoming an independent research and policy consultant in 1987. In this consultancy, he specialises in the application of social research and consensus building to environmental issues. Trained as an environmental mediator and participation practitioner, he regularly teaches an MSc course at the University of Edinburgh and leads training courses in consensus building and public participation for environmental agencies in Britain and overseas. He chairs the Scottish Mediation Network's environmental mediation initiative and is also an active member of the International Association for Public Participation. He is the author of *Resolving Environmental Disputes: from conflict to consensus,* published by Earthscan in April 2005.

David Semple is the Chairman of Catalyst Mediation Ltd, the mediation service and training provider. He was accredited as a mediator by

CEDR in 1994 and is on the Board of the Scottish Mediation Network. He was a commercial solicitor for over 30 years, a founder partner and Chairman of Semple Fraser, WS, and a Past President of the Glasgow Chamber of Commerce.

Alistair G Stark, DipTP, MRTPI is one of the most experienced planners in Scotland, with a background in strategic planning, housing issues and rural community development. Now a self-employed planning mediator, he previously worked in local authorities in the north-east of Scotland and as a planning consultant. He serves on the General Assembly of the Royal Town Planning Institute and is a Past Convenor (2007) of the RTPI Scottish Executive Committee.

Morag Steven trained as a mediator in 1999 and works part time as a mediator for SACRO's East Lothian Community Mediation Service. Since 1999 she has been involved in developing Scottish SEN/ASN mediation, resolving educational disputes and delivering training and information sessions to schools and education authorities. Morag is a member of the Advisory Group of the ESRC project on Dispute Resolution in Education in Scotland and England which will produce its report in late 2009. A board member and director of the Scottish Mediation Network, and co-chair of SMN's ASN Mediation Initiative Group, Morag is also a sessional conciliator with the Disability Conciliation Service across the UK.

John Sturrock, QC is founder and Chief Executive of Core Solutions Group and has mediated in a wide range of disputes in the public and private sectors in the UK and abroad. He is listed in Band 1 in the Best of UK Mediators in the 2008 Chambers Guide to the UK Legal Profession and is an internationally recognised trainer and facilitator in negotiation, mediation and communication, working with athletes, parliamentarians and senior executives together with lawyers and other professionals. He was Director of Training and Education in the Faculty of Advocates from 1994 to 2002, leading the Scottish Bar's award-winning advocacy skills programme. He became Queen's Counsel in 1999 and is a Visiting Professor at Strathclyde University.

Chapter 1

MEDIATION IN SCOTLAND IN 2008 — AN OVERVIEW

John Sturrock

Significant progress has been made in Scotland in recognising the potential for mediation to help people, organisations and others to address disputes and differences. The first family mediation services were set up in Scotland in the 1980s. Community mediation began to emerge in the 1990s, as did civil and commercial mediation providers. Since the turn of the millennium, mediation has become much more topical than ever before. However, there remains much to be done to embed mediation across the whole range of activities in which it has a role to play and to encourage users and policy-makers to have confidence in the process.

THE SCOPE FOR MEDIATION

Mediation can be used in all manner of settings: families separating, neighbours in conflict, where partnerships or alliances are being put together in the public or private sector, where scarce financial and other resources are being allocated among diverse interests, when ongoing public and other projects need management assistance, when commercial and other deals may become stuck, when communities of all sizes are in jeopardy, where deprivation extends beyond the merely economic to the need to find a way to communicate, and when our fragile environment faces competing claims for its use. All can benefit from the involvement of a skilled, independent third party whose impartiality can induce trust and the capacity to build bridges.

THE BREADTH OF MEDIATION

It is clear that, in many jurisdictions, the courts and legislature have played important leadership roles in promoting the use of mediation as an "alternative" to traditional litigation and to the adversarial system generally. Often in other parts of the world, mediation champions have emerged in the senior judiciary or among policy-makers. That has not yet been the experience in Scotland. But this may also represent an opportunity. Mediation is not a mere alternative to litigation: the term "alternative dispute resolution" is confusing and outdated. It is a much broader expression of the hopes and aspirations of so many who seek an opportunity to be heard, to explore the real issues which underlie the superficial symptoms in a conflict, to identify the possibilities and options for moving forward, and to have their say in the outcome of difficult problems that they face.

In the context of litigation, a senior US judge, Wayne Brazil, has described this as the "democratisation" of the court system. But mediation can go much further than that. Mediation offers the opportunity to give a genuine voice to people in situations in which differences arise. It offers the prospect of useful dialogue, enlightened understanding and creative solutions across the widest span of human activity. If Scotland can avoid an overly litigation-based or legalistic orientation of mediation (as is occurring elsewhere) and maintain it as a free-standing, generally voluntary option for those who wish to use it, we can continue our journey down a broad and ultimately more fulfilling path.

REVIEW OF THE CIVIL COURTS

In the Spring of 2009 we will learn the outcome of the review, chaired by Lord Gill, into the civil court system in Scotland. Mediation merited significant coverage in the consultation paper issued by the review group. It will be interesting to learn what view is taken in subsequent proposals of the role that mediation can play in and alongside the court system. Hopefully, it will be given the support and encouragement it has received in so many other jurisdictions from leading judges. The Scottish Government is now well informed about mediation and has supported efforts to promote mediation through the Scottish Mediation Network and the Scottish Mediation Register.

WHAT DO WE MEAN BY "MEDIATION"?

There is a difficulty here. "Mediation" is a well-used word and appears to be understood by many. In reality, it means different things to different people, depending upon background, culture and inclination. To many more, it means nothing at all. In a debate on "alternative dispute resolution" in the Scottish Parliament in November 2007, the importance of retaining the distinctive character of mediation in contrast with that of arbitration was highlighted.

To some, "mediation" carries with it connotations of weakness and soft compromise; mediators and others do have to wrestle with these issues. It presents challenges to find ways to describe and promote the value of an independent facilitator who has the skill to guide parties through a process which is both informal and structured and who is understood not to be a decision-maker. Perhaps not least of these is to decide whether within the definition of "mediation" is included any, some or all of a number of possibilities: informal problem-solving, group facilitation, collaborative negotiation, public dialogue, consensus building, victim—offender conferencing and reconciliation, just to give examples of other recognised conflict resolution techniques. If the same legislative protection for the confidentiality of the mediation process, as has existed for a number of years for family mediators, is to be extended more broadly, this is a real issue.

MEDIATION STANDARDS AND PRACTICE

There is also the challenge of ensuring, so far as is possible, that this emerging mediation profession is not compromised by such a lack of competence that confidence in and the validity of mediation are called into question. That remains a risk while there is no uniform regulation of standards; however, to seek such uniformity is likely to be both an impossible task and damaging to such a diverse and multi-faceted profession. Setting uniform competency standards may be inappropriate for such a diverse discipline. And yet the International Mediation Institute has established an International Standards Commission to address this very question globally. This issue will not disappear. Meanwhile, it is incumbent upon everyone in the mediation world to aspire to the highest standards of ethics and competence.

In the context of ethics and competence, one might reflect on the differing practices of mediators. Mediators often distinguish the facilitative from the evaluative models. In reality, of course, there is a continuum or spectrum within which mediators work. But there are risks when the range of approaches is wide, so much so that the behaviour of a mediator in a commercial dispute, say in Texas, may be almost unrecognisable from that of a mediator in a Scottish "stair-heid rammy" (neighbour conflict). Neither approach may be wrong or unexpected but the importance of understanding context and circumstance and being skilled and astute enough to act accordingly may well determine how well mediation thrives. There are so many ways in which mediation can be done well. And just as many ways in which it might be done badly.

THE VALUE OF MEDIATION

Again, mediators face a paradox when promoting the value of mediation. We are in a position to offer a service which has the potential to save or reduce cost to a substantial extent, whether in pure economic terms or in the avoidance or alleviation of distress, anxiety and loss of morale; in the preservation of reputation and saving of face and dignity; in the reduction in the passage of time spent in unremitting polarisation; or in mending broken relationships — personal, professional, business or community. Yet mediation as a service is regularly undervalued or not valued at all. It is difficult, if not impossible, to conduct a conventional cost–benefit analysis of mediation. The alternatives to healing, reconciliation, resolution or settlement are almost always unquantifiable in immediate financial terms. But one hopes that the time will come when the growing understanding of what underlies mediation will cause sceptics and cynics to accept what those who observe closely already know: that the mediation process is a remarkable tool for adding value, managing cost and risk and, in crude monetary terms, enhancing the bottom line.

ENHANCING THE USE OF MEDIATION

If the wish is to grow a wealthier, healthier, fairer, stronger, safer, greener, smarter Scotland, then I believe that mediation can play a role across the board. Consider its role in economic dialogue and business matters. As a mediator in a wide range of commercial matters, I have frequently seen seemingly intractable, long-running disputes brought to a conclusion in a day or less. This could be replicated elsewhere. For example, there is scope to do so much more in the NHS in Scotland, where the pilot project in medical negligence claims has been remarkably under-used, and where other tensions between and among medical practitioners and hospitals could be addressed to the benefit of the service and patients. Similarly, deep-seated management, human resource and workplace problems can be resolved in remarkably short periods of time using mediation. Issues of discrimination and inequality are also well suited to this private and thoughtful process where underlying concerns can be brought to the surface in a non-confrontational manner.

A NEW APPROACH

Dealing with disputes and difficult situations is usually about more than someone's formal or legal rights. It is usually about a deeper quest to understand the frailties and vulnerabilities, the aspirations and needs, and the concerns and objectives of individuals, organisations, businesses and communities. Mediation represents a move away from the win/lose, right/wrong logic of polarised conflict. It might be said that it is also about moving from what may be perceived as a paternalistic approach to problem-solving, towards a more collaborative, empowering approach — an approach where greater responsibility and control are given to those whose difficulty is being addressed, placing them in the centre of things and conferring choices. Among other outcomes, this should cause us to view mediation as an option that lies outside and which precedes resorting to court, as well as sitting alongside and complementing litigation.

One of the challenges, it seems to me, is to shift our thinking about conflict and its resolution from the frequent focus on rights and remedies. This tends to address problems after they arise or escalate. It is surely consistent with modern thinking, and indeed with the Scottish Government's policies, to ensure that resources are directed towards identifying real interests as early as possible and adopting preventive action. This would help to address problems as they arise or before they escalate. Mediation has a significant role to play here.

For example, sustainability in the environment is already one of the most important concerns of the modern age. Planning issues are intertwined with this and there is deep dissatisfaction at all levels with the current time-consuming, costly planning procedures. Here, mediation — whether as consensus building, public dialogue or in other forms — has much to offer, in policy-making as well as in management of differing perspectives and resolution of actual disputes.

According to Ken Cloke, mediation has, along with other conflict resolution techniques, "amply demonstrated, in countless conflicts over the last three decades that there is a better outcome than winning and losing, a more successful process than accusation and blaming, and a deeper relationship than exercising power over and against others".[1]

None of this is easy, of course. If it were easy, mediation would be a mainstream activity already. The same fears and concerns, anxieties and lack of understanding attend the reception of mediation as are present in any difficult situation where there are differences of view. Mediation, which can help address the paradoxes and ambiguities that cause so much conflict, often presents itself in paradoxical ways which probably result in the ambivalence with which it is viewed.

THE CHALLENGER AHEAD

There is a trend emerging globally. It is represented by the growing use of "third side" processes to address conflict. William Ury's book

---

[1] K Cloke, *Mediating Dangerously: The Frontiers Of Conflict Resolution* (2001).

The Third Side[2] inspires everyone to play their part: "The task is to transform the culture of conflict from coercion to consent and from force to mutual interest."

Ury demonstrates that third-siders focus on how people handle their differences, which is just as important as the outcome they reach. Rather than being the opposite of conflict, co-operation becomes a prime way to deal with conflict. As the world seeks to cope with the extraordinary global challenges of the 21st century, much of humanity's future may be determined by whether this trend towards third side transformation ultimately prevails over the power-based, hierarchical paradigm that has dominated for so long.

The great lateral thinker Edward de Bono captures the need precisely:

> "Our traditional thinking methods have not changed for centuries. While these methods were powerful in dealing with a relatively stable world (where ideas and concepts tended to live longer than people), they are no longer adequate to deal with the rapidly changing world of today where new concepts and ideas are urgently needed."[3]

A JOURNEY FOR SCOTLAND

Mediation is such a concept and such an idea. It has its part to play in changing how we do things. As those who attended the European Mediation Conference in Belfast (organised by the Scottish Mediation Network and Mediation Northern Ireland) in April 2008 learned, it has the power to transform, to reshape and to heal. This book about mediation represents a small but significant step towards positioning Scotland at the forefront of a culture where creative co-operation and constructive handling of conflict are prevalent. It is my hope that the book will capture the imagination of others so that they will discover the value of mediation for themselves and help to populate that path upon which we in the mediation community have set foot.

In many ways, mediation in Scotland is at the start of its journey and the route ahead is not clear. It is certainly a road less travelled, and that makes the journey an exciting one. In some areas, such as family and neighbourhood, mediation is well established. In others, such as commerce, the environment, and in schools, mediation is gaining momentum. And however far we have come, our travelling companions are among the most agreeable that one could hope for. We hope to be joined by many more.

---

[2] W Ury, *The Third Side: Why We Fight and How We Can Stop* (2000).
[3] http://www.debonogroup.com/parallel_thinking.php.

Chapter 2

THE MEDIATION PROCESS

Eileen Schott

There are many different types of mediators and mediation services in Scotland today and this chapter explains what to expect from a mediator. Other chapters will describe how mediation works in particular mediation fields and while there may be variations in the style and delivery of mediation, the core skills are the same.

MEDIATION SERVICES

An individual mediator or a mediation organisation will typically:

- provide information about mediation that is easy to understand;
- answer questions the client may have about mediation;
- allow the client time to consider mediation as an option and an opportunity to help resolve difficult situations.

If the client decides to try mediation, an appointment will be made to discuss the situation, and to see whether mediation is appropriate.

Some mediation services — such as neighbour or family — are sometimes free to the user and others are fee based. Fees will usually be agreed at the outset so that the participants know what to expect. It is generally considered unethical for a mediator's fee to be dependent on the outcome of the mediation.

There are many styles of mediation and ways of working in the different fields described in this book. What mediators have in common is a belief in mediation as a means of bringing people together. Mediators help the people involved improve understanding of events and give them the opportunity to re-start communication based on a better understanding so that the people involved can find a better way to reach agreement on what needs to happen in the future.

The mediation process starts with information about what's on offer and allows time to consider mediation as an option. An initial meeting with a mediator (or, in some services, a case manager, intake worker or a pair of mediators) will be arranged to clarify the issues to be resolved, what has prevented resolution so far and what might be an acceptable solution for each party. Some situations may be resolved by a series of meetings between the mediator and the parties involved (without all parties meeting together) and this is known as "shuttle mediation". Shuttle mediation may also pave the way for a meeting involving all parties face to face.

THE PRINCIPLES OF MEDIATION

Mediation works on the following principles:

1. *Mediation is voluntary*. It is the party's choice, an option to be considered. The party should not feel pressured into trying mediation. It is also voluntary for the others involved in the problem. A mediator can approach other people and invite them to participate in mediation but if they decide not to mediate, that is their choice. Mediation requires the co-operation and participation of all the parties involved and if key people do not wish to be involved, mediation is not an option.

2. *Mediators are impartial*. In many cases people define a problem as what someone else is doing and expect the mediator to make that person stop doing it or make them do something different. Mediators are not enforcers — they do not have any power to make people do anything. It is a mediator's job to be impartial; they do not take sides, give opinions or give advice.

3. *Mediation is a confidential service*. This means that information is not shared without the permission of all parties involved, so if the client chooses to use mediation they can speak freely to the mediator and will be asked what information they want to share. The obvious exception is an obligation to report any serious risk of harm to appropriate agencies.

WHAT CAN A PARTY EXPECT A MEDIATOR TO DO?

Even if someone has not been directly involved in mediation before, they might have a general idea about what mediators do from the word itself: "mediation", like "median" and "medial", is about someone or something in the middle. A mediator helps people talk about what happened to cause difficulties and what needs to happen to improve the current situation.

When communication is difficult or has broken down altogether, people are often reluctant to try talking to the others involved again if previous attempts were unsuccessful or rebuffed. It is natural to be wary. One of the first jobs a mediator has to do is to gain the trust of the parties. Participants need to trust the mediator and the mediation process before they can consider re-engaging with the people they currently distrust.

Mediation is not just for parties in dispute; it is useful when there is a difference of opinion, a stand-off, a clash of expectations, a misunderstanding and/or hurt feelings preventing people from working out a simple, straightforward solution.

HOW MEDIATORS SPEAK

As the mediator's intention is to build rapport and put people at ease, an informal approach often works well; usually, first names are used if this is acceptable to everyone. Introductions, explanations and questions are polite, short and clear, to avoid misunderstanding and information overload. Mediators address all participants on equal terms: they are not conducting an interview or gathering information for a report. Mediators are trained to be aware of the nuances of communication and continually monitor their own and others' verbal and non-verbal contribution to the mediation process. Mediators also try to model positive, constructive communication and are generally polite and respectful to all participants and to each other (when working in pairs).

A mediator's body language should be relaxed and confident as this promotes calmness in both the speaker and listener. The pitch, pace and tone of voice will usually be low, steady and calm, as it would be in a relaxed informal conversation.

DURING MEDIATION SESSIONS

At first it may appear that a mediator is not doing a lot; this is because the most basic mediation skill is "active listening". This means really listening and trying to understand what is being said while paying attention to underlying meanings and importance to the speaker of what is being said. This approach requires the complete attention of the mediator.

Basic mediation skills used during all mediation sessions include the mediator's ability to:

- make people feel as comfortable as possible in the circumstances;
- show an active interest in what is being said;
- reflect what is happening: what the mediator is seeing, hearing and feeling;
- check the understanding of what has been said or the speaker's understanding of what has been said;
- ask and invite useful questions;
- give a balanced summary of what has been said;
- highlight common ground or positive points raised by the speaker;
- acknowledge the effect on the speaker of what is happening;
- highlight what is important to the speaker.

Particularly at the initial meetings, with each of the parties, a mediator will:

- explore what the participants hope to achieve through mediation;
- explore how that can happen and what happens next;
- close with an agreed plan of action, arrangements for another meeting and an indication of expected outcomes.

In each mediation session, the mediator is busy listening, checking out and reflecting what has been said to help everyone involved get a fuller understanding of what is happening.

MEDIATOR QUESTIONS

Some background information is required to understand a situation from the speaker's perspective, so first contact with each party involved may include such questions as:

- What brings you here?
- What's been happening?
- What effect is this having on you/your family/your health etc?
- What would you like to happen?
- What else do you need?
- What is stopping this from happening?
- What is the worst thing about this situation?

- What would need to happen for you to be able to ... ?
- What do you hope to achieve through mediation?

Mediators tend to use a gentle, enquiring approach. There may be other questions about what is or is not negotiable, which is more or less important depending on the type of mediation and the style of mediation being used.

A mediator may also explore or clarify responses to these questions, asking what makes the speaker say X or Y; a mediator may check the basis of statements since generalisations or assumptions and beliefs need to be examined, given their potential to be misleading.

At a first meeting a mediator will often ask "What's happening?" and the response is usually something like "He/she/they is/are the problem. *They* did this, this and this. That's why I/we did that, that and that". People tend to justify their actions rather than talk about how they feel about what has happened. To them, the solution to the current problem is obvious: the other person must stop doing this, this and this and/or needs to change their ways. The message is clear that the other person is in the wrong and therefore he or she must change. This is equally likely to be the response to the same question by the other parties involved.

PREPARING TO MEET

People are frequently reluctant to admit failure, mistakes or wrong-doing and they often forget or play down their contribution to the situation. It is easier to blame the other person and therefore more difficult to contemplate meeting them, especially if the situation has been difficult for a period of time. To help make possible a meeting between the parties directly involved in a difficult situation, a mediator will help them prepare by asking what would make a meeting possible and what would make it easier. The mediator can then help the people involved to come up with strategies to help achieve holding a meeting.

A set of guidelines for behaviour in the upcoming mediation session can be agreed beforehand, to address participants' concerns. Typical "rules" might include that everyone agrees that it is important only one person speaks at a time so that each can be heard, and that everyone speaks respectfully to each other in the meeting even if feelings run high.

The ability to agree to ground rules gives participants confidence in the mediation process and makes them feel safer, as it shows a willingness to co-operate and address common issues and concerns.

It is a useful opportunity to begin to build bridges. An agreement to "speak respectfully" to each other would be discussed first so that everyone is clear about what that means — what precisely is or is not acceptable.

Practical arrangements should also be agreed beforehand, such as time limits for meetings and a suitable venue. Time will also be spent in outlining the issues to be discussed, the range of options available and the practical outcomes desired.

The parties involved in mediation will have agreed who needs to be at a mediation session and the arrangements should be confirmed by letter stating the time, place and venue, giving directions if required and the expected duration of the meeting. The needs of the parties may have been prioritised before the joint mediation session.

In cases where feelings are running high, mediators will often spend time with the parties during the initial meetings, looking at how they can work productively together at a joint meeting. Going over what has not worked previously may help people focus on what needs to be different at a mediation session.

In many cases it is not what actually happened that is the cause of bad feeling, but how people responded to what happened. If this is recognised, discussion can focus on what needs to be different and how this can best be managed and a meeting between the people directly involved in the dispute or disagreement is more likely to go well. In complicated cases, more than one meeting may be required but in many mediation cases one is sufficient.

AT THE MEETING

Mediators have different styles of mediation and may not all work in exactly the same way, but what follows commonly happens.

Mediators greet the parties and show them to the meeting room. After a short welcome and introductions, the mediator will ask the parties to agree to the specifics required to make the meeting go well or remind people of previously agreed ground rules. The mediator's tone is positive and respectful and can acknowledge to all parties that mediation is not an easy thing for people to be involved in.

Most meetings start with an opportunity for each party to say why they are at the mediation. The mediator may say a few words about his or her role and the parties are invited to agree that only one person speaks at a time so that each can be heard. The parties are then given the opportunity to say why they have come to the meeting and what issues are to be resolved. The mediator manages the meeting, ensuring that everyone has the opportunity to be heard and that contributions are balanced, fair and respectful.

MEDIATOR SKILLS

During the meeting the following skills will be used by the mediator:

- *Active listening*: acknowledging what is said by all participants.
- *Open questions*: asking the speaker questions that require more than a "yes"/"no" answer or short reply, often called "what", "who", "when", "where" and "how" questions.
- *Summarising*: providing balanced (and non-blaming) summaries of what has been said, what has happened or been achieved.
- *Identifying underlying issues*: asking questions to explore underlying meaning to help people say what they really mean and make sure important issues are revealed and dealt with at the meeting.
- *Building on positives*: acknowledging, encouraging and high-lighting positive statements or moves.
- *Challenging constructively*: acknowledging what is happening, questioning its relevance and asking for an alternative if appropriate.
- *Identifying shifts in mood and feelings*: enquiring how people feel about what has been said, what they have heard and what has happened in order to gauge reactions.
- *Identifying opportunities for building consensus on ways forward*: acknowledging and highlighting possibilities and options.
- *Summarising and checking out potential agreements* to ensure that they are realistic and practical.

MEDIATOR APPROACHES

Throughout the meeting, mediators watch and listen carefully. They direct attention to what is happening and keep the meeting going by letting people talk, acknowledging and highlighting useful contributions, and encouraging the parties to keep focused on positive outcomes.

As the mediation session is building towards a satisfactory conclusion for the parties, the mediator will help examine the practicalities: who will do what, when and how. The mediator will ask whether anything else needs to be done to make sure this happens as well as to encourage the parties to look at what happens if problems arise later. A key question is: "How do you want to deal with any problems that might arise in future?"

THE OUTCOMES OF MEDIATION

It is important that people sort out problems as they arise and in a positive way. The mediation process is designed to hand the problem back to those who own it and help them to learn how to manage conflict situations.

Mediation provides the opportunity for parties to talk about what happened, to explain what happened and to hear what happened from a different perspective. The process and the manner in which key issues and concerns are expressed allow participants the opportunity to be generous: to acknowledge their own behaviour which contributed to misunderstandings or bad feeling or to express a wish to be on good terms.

The legal system decides rights. Mediators do not judge the rights or wrongs of a situation. Mediation is an alternative to a "win/lose" judgment; a mediator does not usually give an opinion on the merits of a case. A mediator focuses on how to satisfy the participants' needs and reach a resolution they can all live with. This is in stark contrast to a "win/lose" situation where the winner is happy but the loser may not accept losing and may not comply with conditions or arrangements "imposed" on them.

Most people can work out a practical solution quite easily unless they are feeling hurt, upset or angry. Strong emotions demand immediate attention in a mediation session. Calm, rational problem-solving has to wait until those emotions have been acknowledged, discussed and given their place as part of the problem or the difficulties to be resolved. If the problem is less emotive or a mixture of feelings and differences over artefacts such as commodities, boundaries or resources, a mediator will use their skills to help work out:

- what is important;
- what is most important;
- what people are willing to consider, to give up, to trade;
- what options or alternatives might be possible or acceptable;
- what people have in common, such as interests, needs or concerns;
- what they have to gain or lose by using mediation.

A mediator will often acknowledge the feelings expressed and stress the need for a practical alternative to the emotional, destructive conflict. The people involved in mediation are asked for ways to resolve the situation. They are also offered the opportunity to tell the other people how they feel. If one person decides to speak directly to the other person involved in the meeting, it is the mediator's job to help make this possible.

Agreements are checked and re-checked until they are acceptable to everyone and recorded if required. All agreements are voluntary and it is usual to build in a review period to see how the parties manage in the short to medium term.

Before closing the meeting, mediators will often thank people for their hard work and explain the next steps, such as evaluating the mediation meeting which may involve a subsequent phone call or questionnaire.

MEDIATOR TRAINING

Mediation training focuses on how to mediate, with practice exercises in the particular field in which a mediator is interested, for example commercial, family or environmental mediation. Mediators are drawn from many fields and bring their own particular skills and talents with them. A reader who can answer "yes" to the following questions is likely to enjoy training and working in mediation.

- Do you enjoy meeting people who are different from you and who may hold very different views?
- Are you interested in how other people perceive you?
- Do you enjoy working co-operatively rather than competitively?
- Are you interested in what motivates other people?
- Do you enjoy opportunities to discover more about yourself?

Mediation has existed for thousands of years, but has only become a "job" relatively recently. Mediators' styles or ways of working are influenced by their training and by the organisation or context in which they work. But what all mediators share is their use of a process that brings people together to share information in a safe environment and their trust that people will usually be able to come up with solutions and resolve issues for themselves.

Chapter 3

THE SCOTTISH MEDIATION NETWORK AND THE SCOTTISH MEDIATION REGISTER

Ewan Malcolm

In this chapter, you will find information on:

- the background of the Scottish Mediation Network;
- how the Scottish Mediation Register works;
- the impact of the European Union Mediation Directive;
- collaboration in mediation for Scotland.

THE SCOTTISH MEDIATION NETWORK

In the late 1980s mediators came together to share issues of common interest across their emerging fields of family, neighbour and business mediation. They met quarterly to network and discuss in an informal association which they named the Scottish Mediation Network (SMN).

When the new Scottish Parliament first convened in 1999 there was much talk of a new form of collaborative politics. The SMN challenged the first intake of MSPs to adopt mediation skills when formulating their working practices. A well-attended seminar was run which highlighted the need for a staff resource to support the ambitions of the SMN.

Mediation UK (now defunct) worked with the unincorporated SMN to submit a successful application for lottery funding to set up a full-time office in Scotland. Three years of pump-priming funding began in September 2002. A development officer and administrator were employed and an office was set up in Edinburgh. Since September 2005 the Scottish Government has been the principal funder. When the SMN office celebrated its sixth anniversary in 2008, the staff team had grown to five employees.

The SMN is a members' organisation incorporated as a company limited by guarantee and registered as a charity. The SMN is not a

17

mediation service provider. Its purpose is to promote mediation of all forms in Scotland. It believes that mediation is an under-used option in proportion to its proven benefits. The Network's longer-term vision is to embed mediation into the culture of Scotland.

Acting as a focal point for mediators and organisations from all sectors offering mediation services in Scotland, the SMN links mediators to fellow mediators to encourage collaborative and best-practice working. It also acts as a hub for information; SMN's office links mediators to the public by promoting the benefits of a mediation-based approach to conflicts.

The SMN states specifically that it values:

1. working together collaboratively;
2. mutual respect;
3. clear and open communication;
4. voluntary participation;
5. being an inclusive network;
6. financial prudence.

The objects clause of the SMN Memorandum of Association articulates the organisation's aims thus:

- to promote mediation and other related forms of conflict management for the benefit of the public, individuals and society in Scotland and elsewhere;
- to encourage awareness, understanding and appropriate use of mediation;
- to support and promote education, training and research in skills and best practice in the use of mediation;
- to create and encourage links among the various fields of mediation;
- to promote and organise standards of professional conduct and training.

One of the key issues that emerged during SMN's work between 2002 and 2005 was the need to reassure potential users about the quality of mediators. A large-scale consultation, conducted by the SMN, of mediators and mediation organisations resulted in the creation of a common code for all forms of mediation called the "Code of Practice for Mediation in Scotland".[1] This has become the baseline for mediation practice in Scotland, often referred to in Government tender documentation. Signing up to the Code is a requirement for membership of the SMN.

---

[1] See Appendix 1.

In 2005 the (then) Scottish Executive began a strategic partnership with the SMN. The first objective of this partnership was to improve awareness and understanding of mediation and the second was to start creating a framework to give assurance on the quality of mediation services. Broadly, people cannot choose mediation if they do not know about it and if they are considering mediation, they need reassurance that the mediator has achieved at least some minimum standards.

THE SCOTTISH MEDIATION REGISTER

Although there are many organisations in both the public and private sectors that strive for best practice standards, mediation is, like brain surgery and estate agency, at the moment mostly unregulated.

One option to reassure potential users on the quality of mediators is to look at the Scottish Mediation Register (SMR) (www.scottishmediationregister.org.uk). This is an independent, web-based listing of mediators and mediation services who self-certify they meet minimum standards. These standards set benchmark minimums for training, co-mediation and continuing practice development as well as requiring adherence to an appropriate code of practice, a written complaints-handing procedure and suitable indemnity insurance.

As a result of a wide-ranging collaboration begun in 2006, minimum standards for all forms of mediation were set by the Scottish Mediation Register Standards Board, a group including mediation practitioners, public interest representatives, academics, researchers and people with experience of setting standards in other contexts.

There was broad consensus that the standards should be:

- easy to explain without using jargon;
- straightforward to demonstrate and implement;
- respecting of other quality standards;
- inclusive and incremental;
- administered by a credible body.

As at the time of writing, to be a "Scottish Mediation registered mediator" each mediator requires to certify that he or she:

- has a minimum of 30 hours' basic training which includes an assessment from a trainer or team of trainers who themselves have a minimum of 30 hours' direct experience of mediation in practice. Training must include the ethics of mediation, mediation theory and practice, the legal context of disputes, negotiation, conflict management, valuing diversity and at least 15 hours of role-play practice exercises to develop skills;

- after mediation training, has participated in at least two mediations (totalling no less than six hours of mediation) as an observer, assistant or co-mediator;
- has participated in Continuing Practice Development (CPD) and practice support for a minimum of 12 hours each year, involving some or all of the following: training, support and supervision, mentoring, reviewing and reflecting on case studies and peer review;
- adheres to an appropriate code of conduct such as the SMN's "Code of Practice for Mediation in Scotland" or the European Code of Conduct for Mediators;
- has an appropriate system to address concerns or complaints from co-workers or clients. Clients and co-workers must be made aware of the procedures and records kept of all complaints;
- has taken out appropriate insurance for the mediation activities undertaken.

Failure to demonstrate compliance with the minimum standards set by the Scottish Mediation Register's Benchmark Standards Board could result in the removal of the mediator's name from the Scottish Mediation Register. The Standards Board has set out a process for handling concerns which may lead to the removal of a mediator from the Register for failing to meet the benchmark standards. The SMR can only address concerns that a Scottish Mediation registered mediator has not shown that they comply with the Benchmark Standards.

In addition, mediators who are certified by an independent regulatory body such as Relationships Scotland and the Scottish Community Mediation Network are able to have the Relationships Scotland or SCMN "badge" or "icon" next to the mediator's entry to demonstrate their higher standards of practice.

While the Register does not constitute regulation, it is intended to encourage the raising of standards. The job of the SMN office is to host and support a discussion about this common concern.

EUROPEAN UNION MEDIATION DIRECTIVE

The European Union Mediation Directive on aspects of mediation in civil and commercial matters was adopted on 21 May 2008.[2] The purpose of the Directive is to facilitate access to cross-border dispute resolution and to promote the amicable settlement of disputes by

---

[2] http://eur-lex.europa.eu/LexUriServ/LexUriServdo?uri=CELEX:32008L0052:EN:NOT.

encouraging the use of mediation and by ensuring a sound relationship between mediation and judicial proceedings.

The Directive is one of the follow-up actions to the Green Paper on alternative dispute resolution presented by the Commission in 2002, the other being the European Code of Conduct for Mediators established by a group of stakeholders with the assistance of the Commission and launched in July 2004.[3]

Welcoming the adoption of this Directive, Jacques Barrot, Vice-President of the European Commission Responsible for Justice, Freedom and Security, said:

> "Mediation can provide cost-effective and quick extra-judicial resolution of disputes in civil and commercial matters through processes tailored to the needs of the parties. Agreements resulting from mediation are more likely to be complied with voluntarily and help preserve an amicable and sustainable relationship between the parties."[4]

The Directive is intended to encourage the use of mediation by strengthening the legal guarantees accompanying it. The key components of the Directive are:

- Member States are required to encourage the training of mediators and the development of, and adherence to, voluntary codes of conduct and other effective quality control mechanisms concerning the provision of mediation services.

- Every judge in the European Union, at any stage of the proceedings, is given the right to suggest that the parties attend an information meeting on mediation and, if the judge deems it appropriate, to invite the parties to try mediation.

- Parties are enabled to give an agreement reached as a result of mediation a status similar to that of a court judgment by making it enforceable. This will allow such agreements to be enforceable in the Member States under existing Community rules.

- Mediation is enabled to take place in an atmosphere of confidentiality and information given or submissions made by any party during mediation cannot be used against that party in subsequent judicial proceedings if the mediation fails. This provision aims to give parties confidence in, and to encourage them to make use of, mediation. The Directive provides that

---

[3] http://ec.europa.eu/civiljustice/adr/adr_ec_en_.htm.
[4] http://ec.europa.eu/commission_barroso/barrot/media/default_en.htm.

the mediator cannot be compelled to give evidence about what took place during mediation in subsequent judicial proceedings between the parties.

- The provision of the Directive on periods of limitation and prescription will ensure that parties who use mediation will not be prevented from going to court as a result of the time spent on mediation.

- The Directive aims to preserve the parties' access to justice should mediation not succeed.

- Member States (and their constituent jurisdictions such as Scotland) have until April 2011 to convert the new rules into national law.

COLLABORATION IN SCOTLAND

The "big news" is that mediators operating in diverse spheres of conflict across Scotland are working together collaboratively, showing each other mutual respect. Although entirely consistent with the way that mediators encourage others to act, it still takes perseverance by all to balance the tensions of their competing needs. The SMN has been able to create an environment on neutral ground where mediators can have forward-looking conversations. While the SMN cannot be completely impartial, the mediation community in Scotland has allowed it to facilitate these conversations.

Bringing practitioners from different backgrounds together has allowed people to discover that they have more in common than divides them. Commercial mediators can talk about practice issues with community mediators; environmental mediators can discuss conflict theories with family mediators, and so on. This is no Utopian dream — the reality is rigorous and innovative. Collaborative working takes commitment and focus. This co-operation has informed and will continue to inform the development of quality assurance measures for mediation in Scotland.

No assumptions are made about the outcome of this work to create a quality assurance framework and the SMN has no preconceptions about how this collaborative process will conclude. Learning from experience, pragmatic Scots will insist that a Scottish quality assurance scheme is simple, practical and sustainable. Costs will have to be proportionate and address the need to include volunteer mediators.

By 2010 the SMR may be looking at how benchmark standards fit with those in the rest of Europe. Already, this iterative process has been enhanced by contributions from around the world; for instance, Mediation Institute Ireland has an instructive model. Things will certainly be different in three years. The hope and expectation is that the pioneering work hosted by the SMN in setting minimum quality standards will be a launch pad for further useful developments.

Chapter 4

COMMERCIAL MEDIATION

David Semple

Commercial mediation encompasses dispute resolution in many different areas. A dispute suitable for commercial mediation typically arises from some form of organisational or business transaction or activity. Community (neighbour) mediation, family mediation, peer mediation or additional support needs mediation would not normally fall within this definition. However, there can be overlaps with some types of mediation: environmental and planning, court-annexed, and employment issues can fall within the scope of "commercial" mediation.

It is almost easier to say what "commercial" mediation is not rather than what it is. But typically where commercial mediation differs from other types of mediation is that in commercial mediation:

- the parties are usually accompanied by at least one professional, such as a solicitor or other adviser;
- parties often wish that at least one of the mediators (there are normally two mediators in a commercial mediation) should have experience in the area of the dispute. For example, surveyors or engineers are preferred for construction disputes; employment experts are preferred for Human Relations disputes. This distinction does not necessarily pay due regard to the over-riding importance of mediation skills, but it is, nonetheless, often a client's preference;
- there is sufficient money (as opposed to value) in the issues at stake that the mediators tend to be paid for their efforts;
- sometimes, a quite sophisticated and detailed business agreement emerges from the mediation which takes time to draft after agreement in principle is reached.

CASE STUDY

Printers Ltd was a small family firm which had been in business for many years. It was proud of its reputation and record over two generations. Its customer, the local tourist board, was working hard to boost visitor numbers to the area. Although web pages were becoming increasingly popular, hard-copy brochures were seen as a key part of the marketing exercise so Printers Ltd had been commissioned to print the brochure for the coming tourist season. The tourist board would collect all the relevant information and supply it to Printers Ltd who would produce the brochure.

The brochure was late in arriving from Printers Ltd for distribution. There were numerous errors: wrong phone numbers for B&Bs, addresses mixed up and hotels in the wrong section. Altogether not a quality product, in the view of the tourist board. This led to non-payment by the tourist board of £85,000 of the bill from Printers Ltd. Negotiations went nowhere, so Printers Ltd raised an action in the sheriff court for payment. After many months occupied by various procedural hearings without any apparent progress and with a proof (hearing of the evidence) still many months away, the parties agreed to try mediation.

When the parties arrived at the mediation, they were led to separate rooms where the mediators (there was a lead mediator and a co-mediator) had an introductory discussion with each group. Printers Ltd was represented by two of the family directors and its solicitor, and the tourist board was represented by its Finance Director, Senior Manager and its solicitor, making a total of six people involved in the mediation. The mediators asked the parties to sign the "Agreement to Mediate" which had previously been agreed by the solicitors. The parties were then invited to gather together in one room for the mediation. The atmosphere was very tense.

The lead mediator gave the parties a summary of his role and that of the co-mediator and the way in which the day would be likely to run, reminding the parties of the key elements, such as confidentiality and the voluntary nature of the mediation. Printers Ltd agreed to open by explaining its position. It was clear that very bad blood had been generated by the dispute. The small family company was bitterly angry at what it saw as the incompetence and attitude of the tourist board. It felt that its integrity had been besmirched unjustifiably through no fault of its own and the tourist board was using its position to bully it. It was entitled to its money and intended to have it paid.

In turn, the tourist board said that it had placed great faith in Printers Ltd and that it had been badly let down by poor workmanship, lack of continuity of service and plain bad practice. It had been made to look really bad in times which were not easy for the tourist trade. The money demanded was not due as Printers Ltd had not held to its side of the contract.

All of these sentiments were expressed in the opening joint meeting which felt like barely contained warfare. After each party had vented for some time (in a controlled fashion, being encouraged by the mediators not to interrupt and to show respect for the others), they agreed with the mediators that it might be helpful to move to separate rooms for private meetings with the mediators.

The first private discussions between Printers Ltd and the mediators revealed that Printers Ltd had been reliant on information being supplied by the tourist board which, it claimed, had been inadequate, inaccurate and late, making the job of printing, never mind producing on time, nearly impossible. It gave examples of information with which it had been supplied and which was incorrect. It said that it was impossible to work with these people. It had tried its best but it could not "make the bricks without straw". It managed to get the brochure out with difficulty because of its superhuman efforts and was entitled to the £85,000 it was suing for.

A contrasting picture emerged from the first private meeting with the tourist board. It had been "pure as the driven snow". There was no reason why Printers Ltd, who turned out to be incompetent, could not have done what it was asked to do. Although it was entitled to some reimbursement for the work done, it certainly was not entitled to it all in view of the mistakes, delay and embarrassment which had been endured.

As the day progressed, it became apparent in private meetings with Printers Ltd that two members of the family had been quite ill during the period in question and it had been difficult from time to time to serve its customers fully. It conceded, in confidence, that this may have made the difficulties created by the tourist board worse. It explained the complex process of assembling such a brochure and the logistical issues in putting it all together on its equipment, which, it emerged, was rather aged and inflexible by modern standards. It indicated that operational relationships with the tourist board had become so bad that communications had been strained and that this had not been conducive to achieving a good result. It also became apparent, on enquiry by the mediators, that the hole in its cash flow was badly affecting relationships with Printers Ltd's bank.

In further private meetings with the tourist board, it became apparent that it did not quite appreciate the extent to which the resignation of its manager and some changes in the personnel handling the supply of information for the brochure at its end impacted on the execution of the brochure. It admitted to the mediators that assembling accurate information in good time from all the guest houses, hotels, B&Bs, leisure facilities and so on had been more of a challenge than it had anticipated. Flow of information to Printers Ltd had not been all it might have been. When the mediators presented it with the raw information that had been supplied to Printers Ltd and which resulted in incorrect entries, it had to agree that not all the fault lay with Printers Ltd. Further examination of its position with the mediators revealed that the prolonged court case was not doing its reputation any good with its funders and, indeed, that this whole saga might be prejudicing its future.

After the mediators had explained to each party separately the problems encountered by the other (to the extent to which each party had agreed the mediators could divulge, not including their respective areas of perceived vulnerability), the mediators suggested they might find it useful to discuss together how some of the difficulties might have been overcome.

The parties met together again and had a good discussion, where understanding was expressed by each party to the other of the challenges they had faced and how the breakdown in relationships had made the job almost impossible to complete satisfactorily. At the end of the discussions they had a much better view of where communication had broken down and the reasons. There was open acceptance by both sides that they might have handled the situation better. They agreed to settle the court action at a figure less than that sued for but at a level satisfactory to both sides.

Significantly, the parties were seen after the mediation, having a beer in the hotel bar and discussing the possibility of doing business the following year now that they knew how they worked respectively and their requirements for production of a successful brochure: an outcome unthinkable only eight hours previously.

WHEN CAN MEDIATION ASSIST?

Commercial mediation can take place at any time in the course of a conflict: before it has reached court or, indeed, at any stage during a court action. In the case study, the court case had been going for some time before the parties decided to mediate. The suggestion of mediation at an early stage is sometimes helpful in enabling early dispute resolution. Often, however, one of the parties is not inclined to negotiate, far less mediate, early on. He may need time to have his mind concentrated on the realities of a refusal to negotiate. It may require a solicitor's letter with threat of court action or, indeed, a court action to be raised to bring a party to the negotiating table.

Even this may not be the right time. Only after it has dawned on the parties that court or tribunal proceedings may take a long time, be confusing, draining of personal and financial resources, with an outcome that is in the hands of a third party (the judge, tribunal chairman or arbiter), might they be receptive to the idea of mediation where they might be more likely to succeed with the aid of an independent and impartial person (the mediator).

WHAT ARE THE POSSIBLE ADVANTAGES OF COMMERCIAL MEDIATION?

Statistics from various mediation providers around the world regularly indicate that in excess of 80 per cent of commercial mediations achieve a mutually acceptable outcome where previous negotiations have failed. The most common reason quoted for this is that a trained, independent mediator can assist the parties to focus on their future interests, while leaving the outcome entirely in the parties' hands.

Commercial mediation rarely takes more than one full day, so it can provide a speedy resolution of the conflict. The time taken to organise and prepare for the mediation is determined by the parties, together with their advisers, working with the mediation provider. The speed of resolution often rapidly relieves businesses and their managers of the backward-looking, tiresome and often worrying process of reviewing what happened in the past in order to fight a long court case, and allows them to concentrate on current and future business. Businesses which have been involved in mediation consistently observe that this element of saving is one of the most valuable (but difficult to quantify) benefits of early settlement.

The parties, not a judge or an arbiter or tribunal chairman, decide the solution, so the parties are free to think of what resolution terms are truly in their interests as well as considering what their strict rights may be. The legal background is, naturally, important and often features heavily in commercial mediations, but often it is not the overriding issue for the parties. The parties retain control over the mediation procedure and also over the outcome.

Mediation usually provides a reality check for the parties. Where a court case has been raised or is being contemplated, often the enthusiasm to make a point can cause the parties to overlook tough realities — such as the validity of a contract or the reliability of a witness — that will be crucial in a trial. A mediator is likely, in private and with sensitivity, to give the parties the opportunity to review at their own pace their true strengths and weaknesses. Sometimes it is easier for a disputant (and their adviser) to consider these tough realities with an independent person in private. It often takes a little while in conversation with a mediator for these issues to become palatable.

Another advantage of mediation is that it creates the possibility of creative and forward-looking solutions. The parties are free to look at solutions which are outside the scope of a judicial judgment and avoid the need to focus on the past and/or strictly legal remedies. With the help of the mediator they can think creatively and consider solutions which can influence future dealings positively. This is an aspect of mediation which has received universal approval from commentators (including judges) in contrasting mediation with what the courts can consider. The judicial process is bound to look in the rear-view mirror at the facts that have occurred and apply the law to these. Mediation can and does encourage the parties to look forward.

As illustrated in the case study, mediation enables the possibility of continuing satisfactory business relationships. Parties rarely do further business after a court case is over. This is not the experience following mediations where sometimes a future relationship is encouraged by a solution which embraces that possibility.

COSTS

The expense of organising a commercial mediation and providing a choice of suitable mediators will be made clear by the mediation provider in advance of any commitment. In nearly all cases, the fees will represent a small percentage of the legal costs that could be involved if the case proceeded to a proof (hearing).

APPROACHING THE OTHER PARTY AND SETTING UP A MEDIATION

People may be concerned that suggesting mediation could be thought of as a sign of weakness. Experience shows that agreeing to try mediation displays neither weakness nor strength — more a common sense approach to achieving a settlement before the full costs and risks of litigation are incurred. The party who perceives himself to be stronger should have little to fear from a continuation or resumption of negotiations. If one side considers itself to be in a weaker position, there may be very real benefit in exploring the options for an early and certain settlement. Usually the parties share the costs of mediation equally. Occasionally the financially stronger party (for example, in matters relating to employment, the employer) may offer to pay all the costs of the mediation. An approach to suggest mediation can be made through a solicitor or through a mediation provider.

The mediation itself can be organised by a commercial mediation provider who will give all the information needed about the process.

The provider will usually also offer to hold meetings with each party in advance of the mediation meeting so that everyone can be properly prepared, briefed on the process and what to expect, and they can work out their real needs and objectives. For example, parties may be encouraged to reflect on what might be the options for resolving the dispute, paying attention to costs, timescales and other implications. The Scottish Mediation Register can be a useful source of information about mediators experienced in different sorts of disputes.

It is helpful to prepare in advance:

- a factual summary of the case;
- a short statement outlining the type of work/business of each party;
- a chronology of events;
- a note of the people involved;
- an outline of the legal issues;
- an outline of the factual issues;
- a note of common ground and differences;
- a chronology of the negotiation history up to the last offer;
- the court/tribunal/arbitration timetable and the related likely costs, should the dispute remain unresolved;
- a list of key documents.

These will all assist each party to work out what they want out of mediation and make it much easier for the mediators to get a good understanding of the case quickly.

VOLUNTARY AND CONFIDENTIAL

Commercial mediation, as with all mediation, is voluntary and "without prejudice". The process is, essentially, a facilitated negotiation and so proceeds as any other normal negotiation which either party can leave at any time. It also enables confidentiality, thus avoiding publicity at a court hearing. The whole process, as well as the outcome, is generally conducted in complete privacy and confidentiality.

AGREEMENT TO MEDIATE

In commercial mediations, the parties, usually advised by solicitors and in discussion with the mediation organiser, determine what the mediation process and timescales will be, where it will be held and who will attend. Confirmation will also be given that the representatives of the parties will have authority to agree to the outcome. This is then written into a document, the "Agreement to Mediate", which incorporates other clauses relating to confidentiality and agreement not to use outside the mediation the information exchanged within it, and is signed by all participants.

BALANCING LEGAL RIGHTS, COSTS AND INTERESTS

Any lawyer who has run a litigation case involving files many inches, or even feet, deep knows that costs for the client can rocket and delays abound. Very often, client and lawyer alike wonder how on earth to stop the apparently endless drain on resources of manpower and cash required to see the litigation through. It becomes like a game of poker: who will fold first?

However, this does not mean that the factual (any less than the legal) minutiae are jettisoned in mediation. It does mean that these elements of the dispute assume different proportions in the minds of the parties as they consider what actually happened (which is not necessarily included in the formal papers) and what they truly need out of the situation in which they find themselves.

Although it is important that the parties and their advisers have a good grasp of the facts and law surrounding the dispute, mediation allows the parties, even in large cases, to set their own priorities between commercial and legal issues. This rarely requires a full evaluation of every last detail. In other words, decisions are made not simply on grounds of legal right and entitlement or of cost. In mediation, the parties have the opportunity to balance their own interests against the realities of what they are facing. The way in which mediations are conducted provides the platform that enables this balancing to take place.

WHO SHOULD ATTEND?

It is important to think about who will attend the mediation meeting. The meeting will be less likely to be useful unless it is attended by someone from each side who has authority to settle the dispute. The question of what advice is appropriate also needs to be addressed. The commercial mediation process is about finding a solution which meets the key interests of all of the parties and only partially about legal rights and entitlement. Accordingly, the parties should work out carefully what kind of support they may require from advisers at the meeting which will be a negotiation rather than a court appearance. The presence of solicitors is welcome as commercial mediation does not leave the law and lawyers at the door. Advisers are often essential contributors to the building of a mutually satisfactory settlement.

Nonetheless, it is as well to ensure that legal issues do not supplant consideration of broader issues. It is not unknown for mediations to be hindered by the presence of too many lawyers. Sometimes a mix of a solicitor and trusted adviser from a different professional background can be a helpful combination.

DRAWING UP OR APPROVING THE SETTLEMENT AGREEMENT

As with the Agreement to Mediate, there are now some fairly well accepted standard provisions that go into a Settlement Agreement and the commercial mediation provider may supply examples of these in advance. These must, of course, be checked: the fundamental and sometimes quite complicated details of what is agreed must be carefully committed to writing. This can take some time to complete and may involve detailed drafting by the solicitors. At this stage the mediator is likely to be able to provide help in the form of reminding the participants about the course of the negotiations and what he recollects the parties did and did not agree.

There is no Settlement Agreement if the parties do not all agree. If, however, they come to an accommodation which is seen by each party to be the best they can practically achieve in the circumstances, the lawyers usually prepare a settlement document which is signed by the parties. At this stage, and this stage only, the agreement becomes binding. Such agreement is very rarely breached as both parties have willingly entered into it after a process which they understand and respect.

WHAT KINDS OF DISPUTES ARE APPROPRIATE FOR COMMERCIAL MEDIATION?

Few types of disputes cannot be mediated. Commercial mediation providers in Scotland have been involved in helping to resolve a wide range of issues, for example: family business disputes; partnership dissolutions; construction disputes from house extensions to re-furbishments of major buildings to engineering contracts; disputing shareholders under their shareholders' agreements; intellectual property disputes relating to ownership of rights; workplace disputes of all kinds, involving disputes between employees, or with employers in the private and public sectors; professional liability claims in the legal and medical and construction sectors; and many more.

Commercial mediation is not restricted to dealing with disputes between two parties and can be of assistance where many parties are in conflict. Experience shows that some disputes have particular features which indicate that mediation would help to resolve them effectively. For example, when:

- personal reputations are at stake;
- the parties wish to avoid publicity;
- there is a need for the dispute to be addressed as early as possible;
- there is high emotion that would benefit from a controlled outlet;
- the parties would prefer not to go through the court process;
- the parties could have a continuing relationship;
- court-ordered remedies would not be enough to resolve the dispute.

However, mediation is not suitable for every case. Examples of cases which are unlikely to be resolved by mediation are where:

- one of the parties is not willing, under any circumstances, to discuss the issue in front of anyone but a judge. This includes someone who may be termed a "vexatious litigant";
- one of the parties requires to establish a point of law, such as the enforceability of a restrictive clause in a series of contracts;
- one party wishes to make a public example of the other;
- an order of court is necessary, such as an interim interdict (although an interim interdict, once granted, can create the space for a mediation to take place).

It is worthwhile noting that a case is not unsuitable for mediation simply because a difficult point of law is involved. Clients often have commercial priorities which are more important than the enthusiasm of the solicitors to prove a legal point in court.

POSSIBLE DOWNSIDES

Mediation does, of course, have its critics. Occasionally lawyers come across cases where their adversary has appeared to use mediation as a way of extracting information which would not otherwise be available or for testing how strong their case is. This is an abuse of mediation which may be identified by the other party and/or the mediator, and the mediation will be stopped right away. Sometimes, the prospect of mediation can be used as an excuse to delay court proceedings for a short time. However, given the short timescales involved in setting up and holding a mediation, this tactic should be "rumbled" fairly quickly.

It has been said that only some of the costs involved in a legal action can be saved by going to mediation, as fairly detailed preparations for a mediation are necessary. This is undoubtedly true, but the experience is that these preparation costs are almost always for one occasion only and not repeated, as it is for a series of court appearances.

When lawyers are asked why they think cases are not suitable for mediation, they often raise concerns such as: "The time is not right"; "The case contains difficult areas of law"; "Emotions are running too high to mediate"; "The issues are highly technical and complicated"; "My client wishes to have his day in court"; or "Suggesting mediation will display weakness". Such concerns are understandable, but often misplaced. The post-mediation feedback from such observers is, usually (sometimes with some surprise), that the mediation was well received by solicitor and client alike in spite of prior reservations.

OPTIONS

Commercial mediations can be set up in various ways. Lawyers should have knowledge of mediation service providers and will often contact providers and make the arrangements, sometimes providing their clients with a choice. Alternatively, the Scottish Mediation Network can provide lists of appropriate commercial mediators and service providers who will normally have their own websites from which a great deal of information about the mediators' experience and mediation generally can be gleaned.

It is important that all parties in a dispute are comfortable with the mediators. Sometimes parties disagree on who should be appointed as mediator. If a party is comfortable about both of the mediation service providers or mediators being suggested, it can be helpful to allow the other party to choose. After all, if the experience, independence and impartiality of the mediator are established, unless the party knows that a mediator is not for him, why let the identity of the mediator get between him and the opportunity to resolve his dispute?

Many lawyers and their clients across the world who have been involved in commercial mediation have been impressed with the process and the results. More solicitors and other professionals than ever are suggesting mediation to their clients as they recognise this can be an important option in helping to resolve disputes. Similarly many clients are now requiring that mediation be provided as an option by their lawyers, as the risks of failing to settle in mediation are low, the chances of settling are statistically high and the feedback from participants consistently positive.

Chapter 5

EMPLOYMENT/WORKPLACE MEDIATION

John Moffat

This chapter focuses on the use and benefits of mediation in the workplace being delivered by professionally trained mediators and the potential positive effect on damaged or strained workplace relationships, work performance and business delivery. On occasion, tense, difficult or conflict-based situations will arise in the workplace and mediation provides a safe, voluntary, confidential and independent approach to addressing these.

The content of this chapter is likely to be of most benefit to employers seeking to introduce mediation to the workplace (be that an internal service, external provision or a combination of both). However, it may also offer something for those with some mediation services in place to review or refresh their current provisions and consider the cost/benefit analysis of using mediation.

The fundamental points for consideration are reasonably straight-forward, though each may have many "follow-on" or spin-off decisions as described further on in this chapter.

POINTS TO CONSIDER

1. How does my organisation currently address workplace conflicts?
2. How much is that costing?
3. Would a review of conflict management produce savings or improve the working environment for all involved?
4. Do we need to introduce mediation to reflect good or best practice and the general legislative direction for dispute resolution?

If a review concludes that a mediation approach would be of benefit, the next key steps to consider are:

5. The right model and provider.

6. Getting organisational support from all stakeholders.

7. Advertising and communicating the existence of and access to mediation.

8. Putting in place the administrative support and monitoring standards.

9. Rolling out and implementing the service.

10. Assessing success and developing the use of mediation.

THE REQUIREMENT TO ADDRESS WORKPLACE GRIEVANCE/CONFLICT

Since 1 October 2004 all employers, regardless of their size, have been required to operate within the statutory grievance procedures set out in the Employment Act 2002. Anti-discriminatory legislation also moves forward at a great pace, as do the overarching bodies that monitor and address discrimination.

More generally, employers normally have internal processes that define the requirement, expectation and standards of employee attendance, performance, conduct and behaviour. There may be an informal as well as a formal route for addressing each of these.

Where an employment issue relating to any of these arises, anxiety, tension and fear for employment are often significant features and can have a negative effect on staff and work. Irrespective of the event or issue that has caused conflict to arise, it is often the case that feelings of fear, bitterness, anger and frustration can manifest themselves into the frame of mind of "fight or flight", both of which can have personal and employment consequences. Where a complaint or grievance is made, good employment practice should seek to address and/or resolve the issue and encourage a healthy workplace and a workforce that is happy to come to work, perform effectively and behave appropriately.

Addressing workplace difficulties makes sound business sense insofar as it helps minimise the possibility and risk of claims of breach of contract or unfair/constructive dismissal. However, employers must show how they have addressed any issues and come to a reasonable conclusion in a fair, transparent and equitable way. It is also beneficial to set in place learning outcomes from the process of addressing these issues.

Employers have legal responsibilities to their staff and are accountable to various statutory and legal bodies for their actions if claims are brought against them. Cases relating to harassment and discrimination can be exceptionally expensive. Any failure to address such workplace issues can lead to intervention from external bodies such as the Equality and Human Rights Commission and cause serious damage to an employer's reputation, generally creating a negative impression of an employer in terms of attracting staff in a competitive workplace market.

CAUSES OF CONFLICT

Conflict, disagreements and tense or damaged relationships have without doubt existed in the workplace in one form or another for as long as there have been employers and a workforce.

Over the 45 years or more we might be in employment in our lifetime, at some point or another we will fall out with or have a significant argument with a colleague, manager or other work-related contact. What has changed, and continues to evolve and develop, is the employer's response to conflict and what causes it. It is clear there is a greater emphasis on the expectation and/or requirement placed upon employers to find more successful and sustainable ways of dealing with workplace tensions and conflict. One of the emergent ways to address conflict has been the growth of what is referred to as alternative dispute resolution (ADR) methods. ADR in its broadest sense refers to any way of addressing a conflict or dispute either on a legislative and/or statutory basis, or more attractively at a much lower level, avoiding recourse to a body that will issue a judgement.

EFFECTS OF CONFLICT

The effects of conflict can translate into significant consequences for both the employer and the individual employees involved in conflict, particularly where it is not addressed or is left unaddressed for long periods of time. Below is a list of possible effects on both employee and employer.

Employee

- Anxiety and fear, or anger and bitterness affecting relationships with work colleagues or employer.
- Increased absence levels, primarily through illness.
- Poor levels of performance or production that may threaten employment.
- Learned negative behaviours.
- Unable to perform as effectively in team-based workflow.
- Personal time and energy spent on going over or reliving situations or arguing with colleagues.

- A negative attitude or resistance to being involved in improving relationships.

Employer

- Poor levels of performance or production that may threaten the business.
- Dissatisfied or unhappy staff.
- Increased absences from work, by the employee and potentially other colleagues in the same working environment who are impacted upon by the conflict.
- Time, resource and energy spent investigating and addressing relationship difficulties.
- The employer being accused of a failure to fulfil its duty of care.
- Employees resigning with the possibility of constructive dismissal claims.
- Damage to the employer's reputation.

If for as long as there have been workplace relationships, there have also been workplace tensions, then it is logical to assume employees and employers ought to try to improve or solve these to create a productive working environment. Improvements to working relationships include investigations of complaints (to varying degrees of expertise), pursuance by individuals of grievances, people sorting it out for themselves, or managers (who may be directly involved) or other independent or neutral people facilitating some form of coming together to address individuals issues, which may include some form of mediation skills.

Sadly it is also true that in some cases, people have been ignored, told it's their own problem to solve, asked or told to "leave it". In some cases individuals have no doubt been given the fairly blunt option of "get on with it or get out of it": in effect, resign. It is also probable that some employees have been dismissed for being perceived as "rocking the boat" or otherwise being troublesome to the employer. That in turn invites ex-employees who have felt forced to resign or been dismissed unfairly to consider external legal remedies to address their claims. While hopefully some of these scenarios are less frequent, we must also recognise the burgeoning numbers of cases going to the employment tribunal.

The questions employers might consider are: are employees becoming more and better informed about their rights and more able to exploit management failings successfully? Or is a culture of litigation emerging in the workplace? In reality there is probably an increase of individual rights and of the expectation placed on employers in relation to resolving disputes and a greater degree of willingness to challenge that. Therefore employers need to assess and quantify the risk and likelihood of a dismissal or other action being deemed unfair and, if it is deemed so, what the cost might be organisationally in hard and soft terms.

COST OF CONFLICT

Cost factors that employers will consider when looking at dispute resolution are: relative cost against the benefits of mediation; success rates of mediation; measuring an increase of performance or a return to previous performance levels of the employees involved in mediation; and most importantly addressing the question: "What level of expenditure is cost effective in relation to the requirements of the employer and to reducing or removing tensions or dealing with arguments and disagreements in the workplace?"

Few employers appear to calculate the cost of the time and resources they expend to address employee conflicts and disputes in the workplace. Neither do they seem to assess the relative success of resolution interventions, analyse the processes that allow staff to raise concerns about workplace relationships, or record how often these arise. Since most organisations do not cost conflict, an initial baseline figure often does not exist. Some basic estimating would probably be beneficial to employers as this will allow other costing calculations to have a meaningful comparative context. So, for example, an employer might seek to consider on an annual basis:

- the numbers of grievances, disciplinary and significant disruptions caused by poor working relationships;
- the amount of hours spent by all staff and managers involved;
- the relative hourly rate involved in each case;
- the cost of any directly related sickness absence;
- the cost of external settlements following a successful tribunal claim (and the need for an organisation to quantify contingent, vicarious and direct liability);
- the cost of reparation claims;
- the cost of internal settlements (compromise agreements).

With more difficulty, nominal costs might be gathered or "guesstimated" to quantify less direct involvement costs, ie the attendance and general health, feelings and attitudes of people involved on the periphery and reduced or lost productivity. Such nominal figures can be vague, but these are impacting factors and do have a cost consequence.

All of these are the hard costs of addressing tensions and conflict. With this information, a basic costing model can be used as a comparison against a range of potential solutions or interventions to address workplace conflict. The primary intervention to consider is mediation. Employers should equally bear in mind the positive impact and benefits, which are often notoriously difficult to fully quantify.

CASE STUDY[1]

A line manager, Sarah, and her junior, Gordon, were part of a 25-strong team working in a key department within a public organisation. Their working relationship had worsened over a period of two years to the point where they each lodged bullying claims against the other. An internal investigation followed, recording a "not proven" decision on both claims, but in the meantime their team's output had suffered.

Sarah held strong beliefs about Gordon's general attitude towards authority and the respect she was due. Gordon regarded this attitude as bullying and felt threatened in meetings. There was a concern by the organisation that, because of the effect on the team, without some resolution one or other of the individuals would have to be dismissed. Mediation was suggested.

A pre-mediation meeting was held individually with Sarah and Gordon, to reduce their concerns about the mediation and help them prepare for the mediation meeting. This resulted in each being better prepared to discuss their central issues and express their desires that the mediation would help them to re-establish their working relationship. A joint, one-day mediation was set up in a neutral venue away from their usual work environment.

The mediators were able to create an environment where neither side felt threatened and a frank discussion followed where Gordon and Sarah could express their feelings about each other's attitudes and behaviour without exacerbating the situation. This led to each making positive statements about the other's professional skills, which in turn led to a discussion about how they could use this level of mutual respect to work together in the future.

A wide range of practical solutions were discussed, including the language they would use with each other to reduce potential mis-perceptions, how they would work together in meetings, a specific project where they would work as a team and finally how they would jointly approach the other members of the team and start to rebuild

[1] Case study provided by Catalyst Mediation Ltd: www.catalystmediation.co.uk.

the lost momentum. Sarah and Gordon also agreed to work out a joint debrief for their employer on the outcomes of the mediation and their commitment to resolving any future tensions that might occur using the skills they had learned.

When asked about the mediation process, Sarah said "I believe that mediation has re-established a relationship which had almost collapsed beyond recovery." Gordon commented that it allowed him to obtain a positive outcome from a difficult situation.

BENEFITS OF ADDRESSING WORKPLACE CONFLICT THROUGH MEDIATION

- Conflict is less likely to escalate.
- Encourages an atmosphere of mutual dignity and respect.
- Working relationships are improved.
- Encourages the management of working relationships to be a personal responsibility.
- Addressing conflict can be used to transfer negative energy into more positive directions.
- Employees develop a sense of empowerment and self-achievement.
- Managers who adopt a mediation approach may become more confident and generally competent as managers and organisational leaders.
- A cultural ethos of finding sustainable solutions develops from mediated approaches, which permeates into all aspects of the workplace.
- It reflects good employment practice.
- Where there are partnership or trade union relationships within the workplace, such an approach is well received and regarded (sometimes as the basis of a partnership model).
- Reduces or minimises the risk of legal action being taken against the employer.

ADDRESSING CONFLICT IN THE WORKPLACE

Conflict is often addressed through rigid, complex and escalation-based processes and structures such as disciplinary, conduct and grievance procedures with which organisations tend to be most comfortable and which have developed over a long time either within the organisation itself or through employment legislation. It should also be noted that these often encourage polarised and self-defined roles and positions (victim, perpetrator, witness and judge) and largely place the expectation for resolution to be made in the form of judgment or arbiter's decision falling on one side or another. In other words: a series of classic "win/lose" scenarios. These outcomes often leave participants viewing issues as remaining unresolved or unsatisfactorily addressed, as can also be their feelings of anger, fear, bitterness and frustration.

Trends in dispute and conflict resolution are changing and it is now considered that effective and sustainable remedies can and should be considered and that successful outcomes can be achieved when conflict is addressed at a lower and more direct level as quickly as possible after it arises and when it is "owned and controlled" by those in conflict. In this way resolution can follow a simpler, more effective, sustainable and also organisationally cheaper route (in comparison to formal routes) and arguably with less likelihood of recourse to employment tribunal and/or other statutory bodies.

The nature of conflict has a tendency in some situations to draw others into it. Sometimes the ripple effect of conflict in the workplace can be serious and have significant consequences for a large number of individuals. As well as immediate work colleagues, it seems inevitable that others will also become involved such as line managers, HR, trade union reps and more senior managers. Of those listed, each in their own way may have the potential to offer meaningful and useful inputs or interventions into conflict resolution, particularly in organisations that invest heavily in interpersonal skills development. It should be recognised that useful and effective resolution can be achieved by those listed but also that there is a point at which in some situations they will not have the professional expertise to address and get the best outcome from the conflict or the issues of concern.

It seems reasonably safe to suggest that an important factor in addressing conflict is a recognition that the skills set, awareness and understanding of conflict resolution has a direct bearing on the outcome of interventions. However some of those interventions can potentially make things worse or escalate matters. The important element is in the key players' recognition of their own skill levels in dispute resolution and the extent to which they can deploy this effectively and/or recognise when and if it is more beneficial to pursue a conflict as:

- a formal matter (discipline or grievance?);
- an issue that can be resolved between the parties;
- an issue that can be managed locally;
- an issue that can be progressed through mediation.

If an organisation recognises a need for a formal level of intervention, the processes of investigation or grievance may be initiated. Experience suggests that at this stage there is little or no routine consideration or comparison of potential costs for pursuing any particular option.

For the other options, the underlying assumption is that the parties directly involved are willing participants. However, usually there are more people involved than just the participants, such as line managers, trade union reps and HR advisers who may have had some input. Where this is the case and when it is identified that an issue goes beyond personal comfort, authority or competency, those involved in making that decision should be acknowledged. A handover of authority is easier when participants feel they have been given recognition, respect and acknowledgement of the input they have deployed to that point. This helps and encourages quicker, holistic and co-operative resolutions.

Employers who do not have access to mediation by way of an internal service or external mediation contract have the option of securing any number of professional mediators. However, where there is not an in-house service or contract, and where no relative cost comparison model exists, mediation may be regarded as a prohibitive cost, or one that is not budgeted for if the budgetary authority to spend lies outwith those involved.

COMPARING COST OPTIONS OF ADDRESSING CONFLICT

Grievance and disciplinary costs

Where a baseline figure exists of the cost to resolve conflict, comparative costs for mediation can be made. This requires employers to look at a number of factors. For the formal disciplinary and grievance processes this is likely (though not exhaustively) to include:

- the cost of the conflict, how long it has gone on for, and the overall effect on the workplace (productivity and performance);
- any associated costs of employee absence;
- management time in drawing together initial documentation;
- employees' time spent in pursuance of the conflict;
- investigator and interviewees' time (potential for travel and subsistence costs);
- management and employee/HR/trade union rep time spent in the disciplinary complaint or grievance interviews;
- management time spent in reaching a conclusion;
- time spent on appeal mechanisms;

- time spent in individuals adjusting to outcome (potential upheaval if one party is moved);
- if a dismissal is the outcome, time spent at a tribunal, defending unfair dismissal claims.

External mediation costs

Where a procurement exercise has resulted in the appointment of a mediation contract there may be elements to that which include access to a mediation provider's website, helpline or other advisory inputs. The contract may also stipulate set costs and an assumed minimum numbers of mediations for the provider. Invoicing arrangements will be agreed and cleared, as will travel and subsistence rates which may include overnight costs. Where there is no pre-arranged contractual arrangement, mediation can be secured through a market search of available providers. The Scottish Mediation Register is a useful resource. Usually mediators charge on a daily or part-day basis.

Additional employer costs involved in mediation:

- cost of involvement of those participating in mediation;
- any backfilling costs in relation to releasing employees for mediation;
- cost of time involved in arranging mediation;
- parties travelling to mediation (travel and subsistence);
- mediation location (neutral venue) costs.

In-house mediators or a mediation service

Some employers have developed internal mediation services or trained professional mediators within the workplace to deal with situations that arise. This requires individuals to have a recognised qualification in workplace mediation skills and practice and an expectation that they will regularly practise mediation. Normally employers provide training for staff to attain the qualification and also provide some form of regular (annual) refresher training.

COST MODELLING

In the preceding sections a range, though not exhaustive, of potential cost factors have been highlighted. For any organisation, however, the primary issue is in deciding whether or not to introduce mediation.

Some organisations may consider that introducing mediation is a natural and progressive development reflecting a business and employment trend. As such they may feel a need or a wish to introduce mediation as a matter of course and the cost implication is one they are not addressing actively, assuming that, as an additional option or tool, mediation will play its part in resolving conflicts.

For other organisations it will, for budgeting and economic reasons, be more important to model and compare the costs. Some quantitive and qualitative research is required to profile and record the existing costs of workplace relationship failure or dysfunction — conduct, discipline, grievance and other dignity and respect-based complaints or allegations — against costing the introduction of a mediation model.

Mediation is likely to appear to be an "on-demand cost" for organisations. However seeing mediation in that way is perhaps too simplistic. The key element of the comparison is what an organisation believes mediation can achieve and the principles behind its introduction.

As a potential cost-saving methodology there is a need to accept that any cost benefit that mediation will procure needs to be set against realistic targets over a realistic timeframe. Measures of success and milestones for mediation may be best set in terms of a gradual reduction in cases going to discipline, grievance or other complaint procedure, and improvement in staff assessment of the employer and the workplace through retention rates and staff satisfaction: for example, through surveys and other staff-based assessment of the working environment.

CHECKLIST FOR DEVELOPING MEDIATION

The following checklist may be useful to organisations considering introducing mediation into the workplace.

Purpose, scope and principles of mediation

An organisation needs to be clear about the what, who, why and how in respect of mediation. Careful and well-researched consideration of the fundamental rationale and relatively detailed planning in the first stages will have marked benefits in the following stages. It is the difference between a coherent and well-thought-out strategy and "making it up along the way".

Organisations should consult with trade unions or staff representatives at a very early stage (perhaps best to have them involved from inception) and look at such options as a staff survey, focus groups, a consultation document and any other form of approach that has the dual benefit of allowing a sense of ownership and advance advertising.

Once information and research is complete and collated there are many benefits of expressing the following:

- A definition of *what*, for the organisation, mediation is, and what it is expected, required, and hoped to achieve in the workplace context.

- Consideration of *who* within the organisation that mediation could benefit and under what circumstances.

- *Who* within the organisation supports mediation.

- What are the general principles of how mediation will be applied in the workplace, ie location of mediations, confidentiality, and the recording of outcomes.

Considering the mediation provision for the organisation

In considering what the right provision is for your mediation service, a number of factors should be looked at and weighed carefully.

1. *Ad hoc mediators/mediation service — as required*

    Many independent mediators or small companies are likely to be available on a case-by-case basis and as need arises. However, knowing how and where to source reputable and properly trained or accredited practitioners is important. It is worthwhile researching what mediation providers are available in the area(s) where the workplace exists. The Scottish Mediation Register can be a useful source of information about mediators experienced in different sorts of disputes.

2. *External contract to provide specific mediation requirements*

    This may be sourced through an invitation to tender process or perhaps some more informal contract arrangement. Then the basic contract should specify the anticipated requirement for mediation, the type of mediation, the standards/qualification expected, the required response time to set up and deliver the mediation, feedback arrangements, the process for setting up the mediation and named contact points for both the mediation supplier and the contractor.

3. *In-house service*

    Workplace in-house mediation services are a relatively new approach which can evolve to become what the organisation needs. However, that is not always the best business approach and the same rigour of an external contract should be applied to the provisions an in-house service is required to deliver.

Assuming that qualified and fully trained mediators exist within the organisation (and the costs involved are dealt with as a separate part of the in-house process) then an internal contract or service level agreement should specify the anticipated requirement for mediation, the type of mediation, the standards/qualification expected, the required response time to set up and deliver the mediation, feedback arrangements, the process for setting up the mediation and named contact points for both the mediation supplier and the contractor.

4. *Combination of provision*

Any combination of the options outlined can be melded together to provide the required service for any organisation.

Using the mediation provider

Once a provider has been chosen, consideration needs to be given on a case-by-case basis of what and who is the best way to approach the mediation. For example:

- Is this a matter that can be mediated?
- Have all parties entered into the process in good faith?
- Are all the parties able to participate, in terms of health and wellbeing?
- Will mediators be seen by all parties as neutral and independent? (This is particularly relevant if using an in-house mediator.)
- Can the mediator be released from any other duties or be available when needed?
- Will the parties accept the individuals?

Mediation practitioner standards

Although mediation is still, in many respects, going through a continuing developmental phase, it is a recognised professional skill and one which normally requires practitioners to hold a recognised qualification. When looking at mediation and mediators it is very important that any mediators, whether freelance or those who carry out work on behalf of an organisation, have recognised qualifications and can provide evidence of having recently practised mediation or have in some other way kept their skills refreshed.

Developing an organisational approach or strategy to mediation

Once an organisation has decided to make mediation a feature of its dispute resolution strategy, it is important that all interested parties and potential stakeholders understand why it has been introduced, what it hopes to do, where it fits into the overarching approach to standards, and expectations of conduct and behaviour in the work-place. It is also fundamental that each stakeholder has a good understanding of their role in creating and supporting a mediation-friendly environment. Stakeholders include, but are not limited to: staff, line managers, HR, TUS, senior management, and the Board.

Encouraging a mediation environment initially requires significant organisational input and emphasis and all level support from the top down and bottom up. It is crucial that all the key stakeholders agree on the principal points of mediation and are prepared to support it publicly and assist with the delivery of getting the message across organisationally. This can be achieved in any number or combinations of ways, for example:

- normal and routine communication channels;
- company website or intranet;
- in-house publications;
- trade unions' or staff groups' publications;
- posters;
- roadshows;
- e-learning or other training events;
- pamphlets/leaflets sent to all staff or readily available in work-place locations.

Support for mediation — administration of process

Consider what is needed in the way of forms, contact points, recording of mediation case outcomes, evaluating, costing, monitoring, and developing the mediation provision. Also look at developing pro forma examples of all of the above and/or electronic alternatives.

Manage and learn from outcomes

Confidentiality and sensitivity about the content and context of mediation are paramount and outcomes cannot be linked to individual cases. However, it may be possible to use very general themes coming out from mediations to help organisations see whether there are particular "hotspots" or types of issues that arise more frequently than others.

A holistic approach

Consider making or encouraging mediation to be part of a holistic approach to organisational conflict and dispute resolution. Most organisations will have their own discipline and grievance procedures. In addition some may have developed dignity and rights at work or bullying and harassment strategies. Mediation often fits well alongside or embedded within such procedures. Where it is possible organisations may wish to think about a joined-up approach and linked strategy.

Follow-up

What can sometimes be missed in workplace conflict following a mediation intervention is that the formal or mediated outcome is not necessarily the end of the process for participants, and it is very rarely the end of the process for managers and HR, and workplace colleagues. It is important to remember that conflicts have a genesis, a lifespan, and a conclusion, but can also potentially be re-ignited. Solutions to address this can include using mediators to do further work with participants and/or more generally with being aware of sensitivities in regards to the re-introduction of individuals back in to the workplace in a structured, supported and agreed way.

Chapter 6

INFORMAL MEDIATION PRINCIPLES AND IN-HOUSE MEDIATION

Fiona O'Donnell

The starting point in many mediation guidance leaflets is that "people do not wish to spend their lives in conflict". The immediate assumption drawn is that conflict is bad and harmony is good. This chapter seeks to challenge that assumption by accepting that conflict, disharmony and disagreements are the very breath of life. They will occur whenever there is human interaction and exchange of ideas and they are not by their intrinsic nature destructive.

If that is so, then what is it that often produces the stoppage of normal life and the huge drain on time and emotions while conflict rolls on? Is it the way in which differences are approached or presented? Or is it the general environment prevailing at the time which can make the difference between good conflict and bad conflict?

The purpose of this guide is in essence to explore the following questions:

- What can we do for ourselves?
- What is possible and how far can we go?
- What are the pros and cons of in-house mediation?
- When should we be calling this "mediation" and when do we need external help and expertise?

This chapter is designed also to provoke thought as to how far informal resolution can go and what it can practically achieve. To set the scene, we have used workplace situations as examples, though the principles can be recognised as being applicable to other areas.

In many complaints procedures or within contractual arrangements there is an escalation model which follows these steps: first, try to resolve locally. If unsuccessful, try again at a higher level and ultimately refer to the highest authority if the conflict remains or look to outside resources. These outside resources can include solicitors, the courts, arbitration or mediation itself.

As the escalation progresses, the matter can become more complex and is often regarded more seriously. This can be because the conflict is causing unacceptable disruption or because more resources are being used to make sure the consideration and determination of the dispute are fair, reasonable and impartial.

WHAT CAN WE DO FOR OURSELVES?

If you are the line manager or a person to whom parties come "to sort things out", what are some of the important core elements? That question is often asked as "What can we do for ourselves?".

We suggest that parties involved in a conflict cannot "mediate" for themselves. Nor should what is done to resolve matters be called "mediation" without thought. At its most basic, a mediation process involves a voluntary acceptance by those in dispute that a third party will be introduced to the matter who will be impartial and independent and who will assist the parties involved in coming to an acceptable solution.

However, the informal stage can be the most important of all. It is a point when parties have a crucial chance to pause and think about their conflict. The issues are fresh in their minds. It is also the point where they may be asked to provide a justification of these actions to another person for the first time.

So if it falls to you, for example as a line manager, to determine what action to take and what is appropriate in the circumstances, it is useful to stop and consider what benefits a "mediation approach" might bring at this point.

TRANSFERABLE CORE MEDIATION APPROACHES

First of all, recognising an opportunity to address a conflict is vitally important. It may not have the importance or status of a high-level hearing but:

- Take into account that this opportunity may be the first time either party has had the chance to stop and think properly. Do not underestimate the importance of this moment. Use it wisely and explore all options. Dismiss nothing. One of the least likely options may hold the key.

- Don't ignore the niggling issues and wait until a big row ensues, but instead provide the time and the environment for matters to be discussed at an early stage.

- Don't give your own view at the outset: ask what has happened.
- Display a respect at all levels. It sets the scene for parties to mimic your behaviour.
- Consider whether the parties would talk to each other about options put on the table.
- Ensure during this informal stage that you make your own role clear so that the parties know what they can and can't expect from you.
- Informality does not mean that interruptions or diversions should be permitted. The informal stage still merits full attention.
- Although this is an informal discussion, consider whether you are the right person to be involved. Have you been involved already? Do you have your own agenda and, if so, is there someone in whom the parties would have more trust and who may be in a position to consider the matter more even-handedly?

An example of where informal local discussions with a neutral third party took place followed by an agreed meeting using these transferable core values is illustrated in the following case study.

CASE STUDY

The circumstances involved the restructuring of a finance department within a large organisation. The department's existing staff mainly provided advice and instruction to other departments within the organisation. New project managers were engaged by the employer to provide a wider and more strategic direction to the department's function. Existing staff had well-established practices and networks of communication within the organisation. Various disagreements arose between existing staff and the new project managers. Both groups agreed as a first step to participate in informal discussions led by an uninvolved and trusted third party. Through these discussions, various aspects became clear.

1. There was going to be an examination of roles and reporting lines to ensure that existing skills were recognised and appropriately rewarded by a "trusted manager" by both sides at a future date. Existing staff had been unaware of this and welcomed it.
2. There were to be training opportunities for the new managers to learn more about the existing organisation. The new managers welcomed this to enable them to be better informed.

3. There was recognition by the new managers that not all aspects of the day-to-day operations could be "project managed" and a degree of latitude had to be afforded to existing staff experienced in their roles. Because of that separation of the various elements, there was also an acknowledgement that actually some areas would benefit from a new direction.

Slowly, the new managers were able to feel comfortable in seeking the assistance of existing expertise and being less strict in the language used. There was mutual agreement that brainstorming had to be built into the development of how these new ideas were best implemented and an opportunity for this had to be in a non-threatening environment so that everyone could feel heard.

It became a work in progress with parties appreciating the need to give respect and space to the others within various boundaries. Gradually an atmosphere prevailed where "new ways" of working were not seen as a threat and "old ways" seen as having a blanket ban.

USEFUL APPROACHES TO CONSIDER

You may say that you do all of the things outlined below automatically, but just think for a second: do you really? What would you expect if you were the person in dispute? Keeping that last question in mind, here are some useful approaches to consider:

- Try to maintain a multi-dimensional focus.
- Consider a neutral venue: would the parties be more comfortable over a coffee and out of their usual environment?
- Do you think one person is more important than the other and, if so, are you treating the problem in that light? Try to separate what the issues are from the persons involved.
- Take account of the positive (ie the benefits and value of a resolution) as well as bearing in mind the risks and costs.
- Avoid assumptions about what people know or should know. Establish with them directly what they do know and base discussions on actual knowledge.
- Put aside enough time without interruption.
- Listen openly and don't prejudge.
- Consider what the parties really want: is it possible, why or why not?

- Just because it's not your idea, don't disregard it. If the question "What would happen if ...?" is asked it may lead to some unexpected results.
- Consider and explore whether what has been raised is really what the dispute is about.
- Do the parties themselves have suggestions and are they feasible? If not, why not?
- Don't discard out of hand the notion that they may not actually need to agree at all. Have things blown up out of proportion or is there room for a healthy debate with the airing of views?
- Ask "Is there anything else?" and listen carefully to what comes out. It may be invaluable.
- Consider whether you are speaking to all the parties involved. Just when you think matters may be settled, you don't want an upset from the wings.

WHAT IS POSSIBLE AND HOW FAR CAN WE GO?

This section attempts to address the questions: can we ever mediate internally, or "in-house", and what are the essential standards which have to be maintained? If parties experience something which is half mediation and half something else then even if it works on that occasion, the distinction for the future may be blurred. To take part in a mediation is a specific and proven process and the expression should, we contend, be used only in circumstances where a mediation is truly what is happening.

Moreover, a trained mediator — whether external or in-house — should sign up to a code of practice upon his registration as a mediator. A code of practice[1] outlines the minimal standards to which she or he works and again it is vital for the integrity of the process that these are adhered to.

MEDIATION CHARACTERISTICS

It is useful to distinguish some key mediation characteristics and what these mean for informal, in-house, or external mediation. These are identified under the headings following.

Confidentiality: who is told

However disputes arise, there will always be pressure "not to have dirty laundry washed in public". The mediation process addresses

---

[1] See Appendix 1.

this by virtue of the confidentiality of the whole process itself and the fact that any matters are only released with the consent of the participating parties. The understanding by the parties of the confidential nature of mediation and their signing of a confidentiality agreement prior to the start of mediation is a distinct signal that this is something quite different from other ways of resolving the matter.

A confidentiality agreement will usually be signed by the parties prior to the mediation. If an organisation has an internal mediator carrying out the mediation, this is especially important. It demonstrates a clear bubble within which subsequent discussions and meetings will take place as part of the mediation. It also signals clearly this is outwith other formal or informal processes, whatever these may be, and that information released will never be recycled for these future processes by any of the parties at any time.

For whatever period the mediation exists there will normally be radio silence and after the mediation is finished, whether successful or unsuccessful, the parties will decide what information is released. The fact of a mediation taking place at all may be part of that information, or the parties may agree to a mediation statement and include the persons who require knowledge of the information for the agreement to be implemented.

For internal mediations to work at all, this must be afforded absolute respect by the organisation. There cannot be leakage or pressure to release information. The parties to the mediation must be able to trust that what they choose to reveal stays within the mediation. If this cannot be recognised and stringently applied, then use of a mediation process by an organisation will ultimately be doomed to failure. In addition, the mediator will be compromised and undermined. This is therefore one of the essentials that has to be carefully considered at the very outset when the parties are thinking whether mediation is appropriate for them.

Impartiality

Unless there is a discrete office of dispute resolution within an organisation then it is probable that an internal trained mediator will have other roles. In a very large organisation with different departments this may not be so much of an issue, depending on what other role the mediator has. In a small organisation the choice of mediator and who can perform that role requires very careful consideration. But one thing is sure: if acting as mediator, that ends the involvement of him or her in any other process which may follow. The trust of the parties in that person as mediator is vital and has to be maintained at all costs.

Who decides when mediation is appropriate?

Ultimately, it is the parties themselves. The process is voluntary so there has to be a willingness on each side to engage. In the workplace there may be certain principles which, from the employer's or employee's perspective, should not be brought forward to mediation and that should be tested in other arenas. It should be borne in mind, however, that mediation, even if resolution of all issues is not achieved (and the success rate is high), can help focus in each party's own mind what the fundamental issues actually are. If policies refer to informal resolution as a first option and there is clear signposting and information available on mediation as a viable option, then a gradual culture shift to this as one of the workable alternatives should naturally follow.

The importance of how feedback and follow-up is achieved after the mediation should also be thought through. Not only might it be important to the parties to be able to give their views but also feedback is important as a way to keep the future direction of informal resolution under review as to what works and what doesn't. It may also be an indication that there is a bigger problem within an organisation if general statistical information starts to show trends.

No-go areas

Cases not suitable for mediation include: when the parties are unwilling; when someone has strongly held principles which they want to uphold; when there are conflicting interests, especially if the dispute involves an organisation's relationship with an outside body. In this latter situation, it is impossible to see how an in-house mediator from one body would be able to conduct a mediation with another outside body. The conflict of interests is apparent. The interests of the mediator in the outcome cannot not be overcome. At this point outside referral is vital. An internal mediator could only represent his own body as an adviser and as a party to the mediation itself. However, there are many situations where an external conflict could be approached using some of the mediation techniques described earlier in this chapter.

One mediator for all and the right to choose

If you adopt the idea that "local is best", then to immediately "go outside" every time parties agree to mediate may not be the way forward. What is the subject of the mediation? Is it appropriate for an in-house mediation? Is there a mediator in whom the parties will trust?

To answer these questions, it is important for the stage already to be set. In order to achieve that, there needs to be a culture of using alternative means of resolution and the incorporation of these as alternatives within policies and procedures. This can be a "chicken and egg" situation. What is it that comes first? Is it a handful of "successful" mediations to bring on board the sceptics in an organisation or a well thought through strategy? Cultures of organisations will vary but in reality it is likely that progress will require a gradual combination of both.

If the parties agree to mediate but do not agree that a certain mediator (either in-house or external) is appropriate, then that is their call. A mediator cannot be forced upon parties. Their credentials and expertise should be transparent. The cornerstones of impartiality and confidentiality should not be compromised.

WHEN SHOULD WE BE CALLING AN INTERVENTION "MEDIATION"?

This really brings us back to distinctions between trained mediators who hone their skills in a professional manner and others trained to adopt some of the techniques of mediation. The analogy here of a general practitioner may be a good one. A GP knows his patients and deals with their ordinary problems on a day-to-day level. At some point there is a judgement call to be made on when the problem is outwith the GP's sphere of expertise and a referral is recommended for the best interest of the patient. If and when that point comes is down to individual circumstances.

Another analogy may be drawn with the introduction of the anti-discrimination laws. When disability legislation was first introduced there was much discussion about the social rather than the medical model. One early example of this was that in some Scandinavian countries when a disabled person had asked where the disabled toilets were situated, there was no understanding of the question. The reason for this was that all toilets were adapted for disabled access and the term "disabled toilet" itself had simply lost its meaning.

If mediation ever came to the equivalent position, it may inevitably diverge into a variety of forms. Provided it remained true to its core essentials, such evolution of "being the norm" would surely be of benefit to us all. Perhaps then we may be in a position to prepare for the arguments to happen, set boundaries and give thought to how to accommodate dissent and give room for differences.

Even if the growth of knowledge of mediation at the grassroots results only in a perception that in Scotland "there is a better place to have this discussion and a better way to express it", that must still be a starting point. From that starting point, there should be room for a variety of forms of early dispute resolution to give space for differences to exist and avoid the meltdown situations.

Debate on whether development areas in mediation should be informal or in-house or as a sibling of external mediation is healthy and should be welcomed from all quarters. There is, however, room for all varieties of mediation in a context of dissent or conflict; conflict being inevitable and actually not being a bad thing.

Chapter 7

MEDIATION IN A
HEALTH SERVICE SETTING

Deirdre Armstrong

This chapter is an introduction to the NHS in Scotland, its size and organisational complexity, a consideration of what people want from complaints about care and opportunities for the use of mediation in the NHS system.

NHS Scotland is Scotland's largest employer, with almost 158,000 staff[1] who apply a continuum of knowledge, skills and experience to a wide range of occupations including: statisticians, economists, librarians, medical artists, chaplains, chefs, doctors, nurses and other health professionals.

Health services are delivered through 14 regional NHS Boards. Scotland has a further eight Special Boards which provide services on a national basis, for example the Scottish Ambulance Service. Each regional board runs the entire local NHS system in its geographical area and ensures that services are delivered effectively and efficiently. NHS Boards are responsible for the provision of care and the management of the whole range of health services in an area including general and specialist hospitals and clinics (secondary care), and community care and GP practices (primary care). Around 90 per cent of patient contact takes place at the primary care level.[2]

The NHS experiences tensions created by the traditions of these evolving health professions on the one hand and, on the other, the increasing political requirement to be seen to be creating more efficient and effective clinical services. Its organisational culture is intrinsically hierarchical and tribal. In short, it is a complex arrangement or set of (sometimes quite vaguely) related organisations. Within such an

---

[1] http://www.isdscotland.org/workforce.
[2] *The National Health Service in Scotland*, Scottish Parliament (Spice) Briefing 07/32 13 June 2007.

environment, it would be surprising if disputes within and about the NHS did not occur.

The following two case studies illustrate first the emotionally charged clinical situations which often occur and the importance of maintaining good relationships when care is ongoing and the value of non-financial outcomes, and, second, an example of one of the many kinds of commercial dispute that can take place in an NHS setting.

CASE STUDY 1: A COMPLAINT ABOUT STANDARDS OF CARE

Mr and Mrs MacNeil had a complaint against their GP surgery about the way Mrs MacNeil felt the surgery diagnosed her illness and also against the local hospital-based oncology service. Mrs MacNeil believed there had been undue delay in her being referred to this service; she felt she had been pushed "from pillar to post" by the surgery, she hadn't seen the same GP twice, and none of them seemed to take her seriously. Both she and her husband believed she had suffered "lack of care" from the surgery. When she was finally referred to the oncology service she felt that she should have gone to the top of the queue for treatment as the delay had not been her fault. However, her treatment didn't start for some weeks. She was now well, but this delay had resulted in her being away from the business the MacNeils jointly ran for far longer than was necessary. This meant that they were under severe financial strain as a family as well as all having the emotional stress they had to deal with. They had suffered unduly and they didn't want the same thing to happen to someone else.

They had written to both the surgery and the hospital and made a formal complaint. When the written responses arrived the MacNeils found the letters unsatisfactory. It was clear that the hospital had not spoken to the GP surgery and vice versa. In their view both were defensive and contradictory; they said they were sorry Mrs MacNeil "felt" that her case had been badly handled. For their part, the general practitioners were disappointed to receive a written complaint and would have liked Mrs MacNeil to approach them directly rather than submitting a formal complaint. The hospital staff were also disappointed. Their complaints manager had already spent a great deal of time investigating this case and they knew that if the MacNeils took it to the Scottish Public Service Ombudsman it would take up even more resources and the outcome was uncertain. The MacNeils then intimated that they were indeed going to take their complaint "all the way" — to their MSP, the Ombudsman, the press and they were even prepared to go to court. At this point mediation was suggested.

Several preliminary conversations took place between the mediator and the various parties by phone and e-mail. The mediation took place over three half-day sessions and included meetings with various combinations of the individuals involved. The MacNeils attended meetings as a couple. Others involved were the NHS Health Board Director with responsibility for oncology services and the hospital's Complaints Manager. The senior partner of the GP practice and the Practice Manager made up a third group. In between meetings, the mediator kept the process moving by preparing everyone for the next meeting and ensured that individuals were actually doing the tasks they had undertaken, such as drafting apologies.

Joint meetings provided the following for all the parties: an opportunity to have their feelings and thoughts surrounding the complaint listened to and acknowledged, a constructive forum to answer questions that had arisen regarding Mrs MacNeil's care, an opportunity to consider the communications systems between the surgery and the hospital, and a discussion about the future relationship between the MacNeils and the surgery. By encouraging reflection, the mediator enabled all parties to see other points of view.

Rigorous "reality testing" of options with the parties separately revealed that the MacNeils had no real desire to go to court (supposing they had a legal case); it would just take more time and they might not win, which could be very costly. They felt they had been labelled troublemakers and that might compromise their ongoing care from the surgery. However, generally they liked the doctors there and it was convenient — if matters could be resolved they would stay with the practice.

The Health Board Director and the hospital's Complaints Manager wanted very much to do everything reasonable to ensure the best possible care for individuals and their families undergoing cancer care. They wanted to learn from the handling of this complaint. With the best possible systems and clear lines of communication in place things could be made better for the future. On a more practical level, the Health Board did not particularly welcome a protracted investigation by the Ombudsman who might well have found that Mrs MacNeil's case was handled inappropriately and such a finding would be made public.

The senior partner of the GP practice and the Practice Manager resented how much time this was all taking. The surgery had done their best. It was impossible to get things right 100 per cent of the time. Perhaps Mrs MacNeil should consider her good fortune: her treatment had ultimately been successful. However, the GP and his partners appreciated that patients could react emotionally to bad news and perhaps the practice needed a better way to share patient information.

A resolution agreement was achieved. Written apologies were delivered from both the surgery and the hospital to the MacNeils.[3] Both the surgery and the hospital were able to respond to the MacNeils' concerns about the perceived delay in Mrs MacNeil receiving treatment and acknowledged the impact that this had had on the whole family, emotionally and financially. They also agreed to action some of Mrs MacNeil's requests about communication between the GP partners and the hospital. The MacNeils agreed to raise any future concerns informally with the GP's who undertook to make themselves available to listen. The Health Board also agreed to review the way it managed urgent referrals to ensure that the same situation couldn't happen again. Outwith the terms of the agreement, the hospital would review how they dealt with complaints. Additionally, a modest *ex gratia* payment was made to the MacNeils, "as a gesture of goodwill" and in full and final settlement of the dispute.

The MacNeils felt vindicated. They now had a genuine apology, which said that things could have been done better. The financial compensation, though not the most important thing to them, acknowledged this. What was more important was that the same thing wouldn't happen again.

The Health Board staff felt positive about the mediation but also found it time consuming and draining. They had heard a lot that was often unpalatable. It had forced them to see things from the point of view of the patient and her family and some things would be done differently in future. Prior to mediation, their sense was that the complaint wasn't going to go away and indeed was likely to be investigated by the Scottish Public Service Ombudsman. That would have taken up significant staff resources, but now the complaint had been dealt with.

The GP and his colleagues were also pleased that the matter had been addressed, however, it was very time consuming. They had anticipated future "issues" with the demanding MacNeils but these had been allayed by the contents of the resolution agreement. So, ultimately they agreed that they could not see how the matter could have been dealt with adequately in any way other than mediation.

CASE STUDY 2: A COMMERCIAL DISPUTE BETWEEN THE PARTNERS IN A GENERAL MEDICAL PRACTICE

The partners of a large general practice were in dispute. Six of the seven partners (referred to here as "the partners") were seeking

---

[3] The Scottish Public Service Ombudsman *Guidance on Apology* was helpful in writing this document.

the departure of one, Dr Ferguson, after a complete breakdown in working relationships. The GP partners had no formal partnership agreement.

With the help of each party's legal advisers, a number of separation issues had already been agreed. What remained in dispute was the amount of the payment to be made to Dr Ferguson and the nature of the separation agreement, ie Dr Ferguson's resignation or the dissolution of the partnership. The partners were reluctant to have to go down the latter route.

The terms of the valuation of the owned premises had been agreed, though there remained some ambiguity about the basis of the valuation. There was also a difference of opinion about the necessity to appoint a judicial factor[4] should dissolution proceed.

Dr Ferguson had joined the already well-established medical practice four years previously as a full share partner for a lump sum "buy-in". Almost immediately, problems and tensions emerged in terms of interpersonal relations, "philosophy" and work performance. However, a nine-month trial period was allowed to pass.

Following a number of interventions including the involvement of the Primary Care Support Department of the Health Board and the local Medical Council, the partners concluded that their relationship with Dr Ferguson had "broken down irretrievably". Accordingly, they instructed their solicitor to write to Dr Ferguson offering an amicable arrangement to secure his resignation or dissolution of the practice involving realisation and distribution of the assets and liabilities. When negotiations came to an impasse, Dr Ferguson's solicitor suggested mediation.

A dissolution of the practice would have implications for the future income of all concerned as there was no guarantee that the terms of the existing Health Board contract would be available in the future and indeed the contract would have to go to tender. None of the partners might be successful in securing it. Dr Ferguson felt that his colleagues did not appreciate the true value of the accumulating asset they had in the building. The partners' ideal outcome was the status quo, minus Dr Ferguson, but if they did have to go to dissolution they would sell the building, be rid of mortgage repayments and could lease premises which the Health Board would, in effect, pay for.

The partners and Dr Ferguson had their legal advisers with them at the mediation which took place over a ten-hour day. Despite the best efforts of the mediator to "reality test" their options, both sides failed to move away from their entrenched views of the justification

---

[4] A judicial factor is a person appointed by the court to manage the affairs of another.

of the deal-breaking payment figure which each had arrived at from an irreconcilably different perspective.

Dr Ferguson believed the payment he was seeking to walk away from the practice and the property (thereby leaving the business intact) was "a bargain". By instigating dissolution of the practice, the partners had created a situation where they all would inevitably incur losses. Dr Ferguson believed he was offering his partners a way out — an opportunity to wholly own the premises, secure the capital growth and increase their profits. This offer came at a price, he felt, and its value was a matter of commercial judgement.

The partners' offer was based on earnings. Had there been a partnership agreement (and there was not), Dr Ferguson would be entitled to one year's notice plus the return of his investment. Their offer represented one year's salary plus an uplift to secure his departure.

Throughout the long day, the mediation process comprised a series of four individual meetings, one joint meeting (but with only two of the five partners present in order not to "swamp" Dr Ferguson), followed by two meetings between the mediator and the advisers only.

At the end of the day, the partners' final offer of a six-figure sum was made with some acceptable conditions. Dr Ferguson held out for a figure closer to his original claim, which he believed had already been offered informally prior to the mediation. The sum now separating them represented 10 per cent of the original claim but it was not possible to reach an agreement that day. However, with the ongoing intervention of the mediator, who facilitated continuing negotiation between the solicitors, a resolution was finally achieved: Dr Ferguson agreed to accept a figure slightly in excess of what had been offered at the mediation in a full and final settlement.

At the end of the long day, the partners were extremely frustrated and thought that it had all been a waste of time and money. But when it did settle later they recognised that it would not have done so without the mediation. Dr Ferguson felt that he had settled for less than he had intended to but it was worth the relief of getting himself out of the practice. He could now move on.

MEDIATION OPPORTUNITIES IN THE NHS

Perhaps the most obvious opportunity for the use of mediation in the NHS lies in the very nature of its business and the service it provides; the millions of patient interactions which take place every year in NHS Scotland do so in an emotionally charged arena. Given that, the staff of NHS Scotland deserve praise for mostly getting it right. In 2006—07, for example, there were only four complaints per 10,000 patient contacts.[5] However, when things do go wrong, they can go badly wrong. It is also known from a variety of sources that in these circumstances what patients often want is:

- an apology or an explanation;
- an assurance that it will not happen again to someone else;
- an opportunity to make the NHS listen, to understand what has happened and to say why it is important.[6]

All these desirables are achievable by mediation but not necessarily by the other avenues currently in place, namely, the NHS Complaints Procedures or legal action for clinical negligence.[7] Indeed, in contrast to these, mediation does not focus on the need to prove negligence or apportion blame. It is a constructive forum to answer questions that have arisen in a dispute. It allows all those involved to retain control over the process and to address concerns as they see them.

RESOURCES AND HOW TO GET STARTED

If you want to resolve your NHS dispute — whether clinical, commercial or employment/workplace related — you can consider using mediation. You can find mediators with a special interest and/ or experience of working in NHS settings by accessing the "Find a Mediator" section of the Scottish Mediation Network website: www. scottishmediation.org.uk. Given the multifaceted nature of the NHS, it may be useful to look for a mediator who has experience in handling NHS patient or clinical disputes.

Within the NHS Complaints Procedures there is, in theory, a provision for conciliation but this has not been taken up in practice. So mediation may be a viable alternative, if requested, as "the NHS Complaints Procedures offer conciliation, *arguably mediation by another name* [author emphasis], as a voluntary option available to both patients and healthcare providers — both parties having to agree to the process".[8] The main benefit of mediation over conciliation in this context is that it is a completely independent and neutral intervention whereas conciliation is part of the NHS Complaints Procedures.

---

[5] http://www.isdscotland.org/isd/5113.html.
[6] "No-fault compensation: consultation document from the Scottish National Party". Scottish Consumer Council, September 2006.
[7] The Central Legal Office of NHSS conducted a limited pilot. This is due to report in 2008 on the use of mediation in clinical negligence claims in excess of £10,000.
[8] "Encouraging Resolution — mediating patient/health services disputes in Scotland". Royal Society of Edinburgh, February 2002, p 16, 4.29.

From September 2007, the Citizens Advice Bureau across Scotland has received funding from local NHS boards to deliver an Independent Advice and Support Service (IASS) for patients and their relatives in their dealings with the NHS.[9] It can offer advice and support about the appropriateness of going through the formal NHS Complaints Procedures or using some other process. The CAB also says that a conciliator or mediator may be available to resolve NHS complaints.

NHS employees who have a dispute concerning the terms of their employment may be interested to know that a number of employment and workplace disputes in the Scottish NHS have been referred to mediation, and the majority of these mediations have resulted in the resolution of the dispute in terms acceptable to both parties.

Mediation offers an opportunity to have feelings and thoughts surrounding conflicts heard and acknowledged. Mediation can also take place quickly and thus avoids prolonged stress, uncertainty and anxiety. These universal benefits are particularly valuable in NHS disputes which can be highly emotionally charged.

---

[9] http://www.cas.org.uk/healthcomplaints.aspx.

Chapter 8

COURT MEDIATION

Marjorie Mantle

In Scotland, a mediation service for civil cases is available at Edinburgh Sheriff Court (ESC). At the time of writing, there is no similar offering in other areas. However, as mediation is available in some courts for family break-up or divorce, it may be worth contacting your local sheriff clerk's office to see whether a service is offered in your area. The services are usually funded by the Scottish Government and while they may be located within a court building, they are independent of the Scottish Courts organisation.

The ESC Service accepts cases referred by a sheriff within the small claims and summary cause limits. A claim up to £3,000 is referred to as a small claim. Between £3,001 and £5,000 a claim is called a summary cause. It is important to note that mediation is not offered for undefended actions.

A mediation co-ordinator is available within the Edinburgh Sheriff Court building, on a part-time basis. The co-ordinator's role is to assist the court when a sheriff thinks that a case may be resolved through mediation. The co-ordinator can be contacted to discuss any aspect of court mediation. He may also be available for discussion on the day of the court hearing.

AN OUTLINE OF THE STANDARD HEARING PROCESS

If you attend ESC in relation to a small claims or summary cause action, there are usually two ways the case can proceed. On the one hand, it may go through the standard hearing process. On the other, the case could be referred to mediation.

The following describes typically how the court process works, but the exact process should be confirmed with the sheriff clerk's office (see Figure 8.1).

71

FIGURE 8.1: COURT PROCEDURE

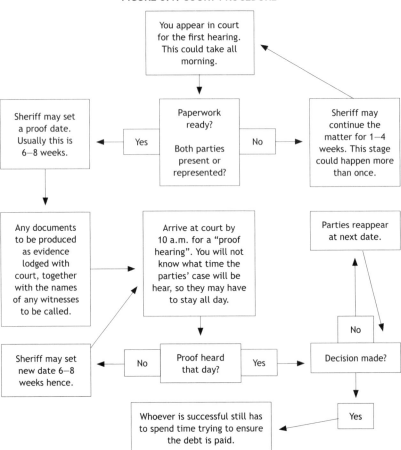

1. When the claim is defended, both parties appear or are represented at a preliminary hearing:

   (a) If all the relevant paperwork is not ready, or if both parties are not present or represented, the sheriff may continue the case for, say, one to four weeks to allow these problems to be remedied. If, at the next hearing, things are still not right or a party is not there, the sheriff may continue the case again.

   (b) If all relevant paperwork is ready and if the parties are present or represented, the sheriff may fix a date for a proof hearing, some six to eight weeks ahead. At a proof, evidence is presented and witnesses are heard before the sheriff makes his decision about who is successful.

2. At least two weeks before the proof, any documents to be produced as evidence must be lodged with the court and the names of any witnesses you want to call. This gives each party the opportunity to see in advance what the other side is going to rely upon so that they are not caught by surprise at the proof.

3. On the day of the proof hearing, parties should arrive at court by 10 am. They will not know what time the case will be heard, so they may have to stay all day.

4. If other cases take longer than expected and there is no time for the sheriff to hear a particular case, he sets another proof date some weeks ahead.

5. If the case *is* heard, the sheriff listens to the evidence presented, either directly by the parties or from witnesses.

6. Once the sheriff has heard both sides of the case, he issues a decree (the decision). This may happen at the end of the proof. However, it may be that the sheriff defers the decision to another day.

7. Once decree is granted, the successful party needs to take steps to enforce it, as the court does not do that.

To read more detail about the standard hearing process, visit www.scotcourts.gov.uk and select either "Small Claims Actions" or "Summary Cause Actions".

THE MEDIATION OPTION

Table 8.1 and Figure 8.2 outline, in comparison with the court process, how mediation in a court setting works.

1. At the preliminary hearing, the sheriff may offer the parties the opportunity to try mediation.

2. If both parties accept the offer, the sheriff clerk immediately gives the parties a time and date for the mediation meeting. It is usually possible to have the mediation within two weeks.

3. The parties attend the mediation meeting which generally lasts about two hours. In approximately 80 per cent of cases, the parties reach a solution for their dispute during mediation.

4. If agreement is reached, the terms are put in writing and signed by the parties before the mediation finishes. Once all terms have been fulfilled, the court case is at an end and there is no need for further court appearances by either party.

TABLE 8.1   COURT COMPARED WITH MEDIATION

	Court	Mediation
Time	From first hearing to sheriff's decision, a minimum 8 weeks.	From first hearing to mediation, usually about 2 weeks.
Scope	A sheriff can hear only evidence relevant to the case. Parties must provide their evidence to the sheriff.	The parties can choose to discuss whatever issues they feel are relevant to the dispute between them.
Control of the outcome	A sheriff makes a decision. The parties have no control over the outcome.	The outcome is completely in the hands of the parties.
Cost	If a party is represented by a lawyer, then professional fees are payable as agreed. If the successful party chooses to use sheriff officers to enforce a decree, there will be a cost for this.	There is no charge for mediation at ESC. Lawyers do not usually attend court-based mediations for small claims or summary cause actions.
Confidentiality	Members of the public are usually entitled to listen to court hearings.	All discussions during mediation are, and remain, confidential.

FIGURE 8.2: MEDIATION OPTION

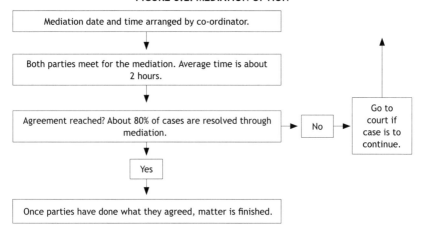

5. If the parties cannot reach agreement at mediation, the case returns to court and continues with the traditional hearing process.

CASE STUDY 1: CLAIM BY TENANT FOR THE DEPOSIT HELD BY THE LANDLORD

Angus was a student who rented a flat from Flora. At the end of the tenancy, Angus asked for his deposit of £500 to be returned to him. Flora sent him a cheque for £100 with a letter saying that she was retaining the balance because Angus left the flat in a mess and that there was a coffee cup stain which couldn't be removed from the kitchen table.

Angus said that he cleaned the flat before he left and that the stain was just part of general wear and tear. When Flora refused to refund the balance of £400, Angus raised a small claims action in the sheriff court. When both of them appeared in court for the first hearing, the sheriff referred the case to mediation. During the joint meeting, Flora was able to show Angus photos of the flat after he left it and a detailed invoice from a cleaning firm. At that stage the parties moved into separate rooms and the mediator met first with Angus.

In the private session, Angus said that perhaps his cleaning skills may not have been good enough to allow a new tenant to move in immediately. However, in his opinion the carpet did not need steam-cleaning and just a good vacuuming would have been enough. He also pointed out that it was unfair to charge him for replacing four tiles in the bathroom because they'd been broken when he moved in.

The mediator then spoke privately with Flora who realised that a sheriff might consider the coffee cup stain to be wear and tear and just one of the things that can happen when someone's been living in a flat for a year. She also realised that it could be difficult to prove that the tiles were broken by Angus. After further discussion, both Angus and Flora decided that it could be stressful and time-consuming to go back to court. Between them they decided that Angus would be responsible for the cost of the work by the cleaning firm, and Flora would bear the cost of the tiles and the coffee stain. Flora agreed to refund Angus a further £75 of his deposit.

CASE STUDY 2: CLAIM FOR COMPENSATION

Mr Jones bought a car at auction for his son. A month later the turbo failed and had to be replaced. Some time later the engine seized without warning and the car became worthless. Investigations by Mr Jones revealed that the car manufacturer, Cars Incorporated, was aware of the problems with this engine type and had introduced an extended five-year policy to cover failures. However, no support was available for cars bought outside the Cars Incorporated, network or without a full service history. Mr Jones alleged a cover-up by Cars Incorporated, saying that it had misled the public by not providing full information. His argument was that a potential purchaser would have no way of knowing they were buying goods unsuitable for purpose. Mr Jones brought a summary cause action seeking £3,150 plus interest and expenses as compensation for the alleged misrepresentation by Cars Incorporated. At mediation, Cars Incorporated said they had no obligation to Mr Jones as he had not purchased the car from them. Mr Jones readily admitted this, but the subtext was that he wanted to give Cars Incorporated a hard time and get some money out of them. He was prepared to follow through with court action if necessary.

During the mediation Mr Jones revealed that he had bought cars from Cars Incorporated over the years because he considered them reliable. Cars Incorporated appeared keen to avoid the publicity associated with court actions although this was not specifically mentioned. The parties reached a settlement agreement whereby Mr Jones dropped the legal proceedings and Cars Incorporated sold him a new car with a substantial discount. Both were winners in this outcome. Cars Incorporated retained a customer; Mr Jones gained a car.

IMPORTANT IN-COURT MEDIATION FACTS

- Mediation is often a faster process than court.
- Usually, solicitors do not attend court-based mediations with their clients. This benefits the party in two ways:
  ◊ They don't have to pay a solicitor for his time.
  ◊ They don't have to discuss legal issues with the other party's solicitor.
- The parties themselves control the settlement terms.
- A mediation can be arranged in days and normally takes a few hours.
- All the party discussions remain private and confidential.
- If it doesn't work, you can still continue with the court case.
- Parties will be encouraged to talk about what happened and what they would like to do to stop the court case.

- Parties will be able to talk through the problems and think about ways to solve them that include solutions not necessarily based on money.
- If you reach an agreement, it is prepared there and then and signed as a legally binding document.

Chapter 9

ENVIRONMENTAL MEDIATION AND THE SCOTTISH PLANNING PROCESS

Roger Sidaway and Alistair Stark

While the value of mediation in the UK is becoming widely accepted in a range of different sectors, such as well-established family and community services, small claims court procedures and a developing commercial practice, environmental mediation is very much a Cinderella in the field. This chapter assesses the current situation in Scotland and the potential for future development of environmental mediation, including mediation in the planning system.

THE POLITICAL NATURE OF ENVIRONMENTAL CONFLICT

Where environmental conflicts differ from personal and neighbourhood disputes is in their public and political nature. They tend to be based on disagreements over policy or the implementation of policy, although personality clashes may also be evident. Many North American writers consider environmental disputes as a type of "public policy" conflict and it is certainly the drama of conflict that makes the headlines.

Environmental conflicts tend to be messy and confused. They are typified by complexity and uncertainty as they contain many issues whose boundaries and participants are unclear. The goals of most participants are incompatible as they believe that they alone represent the public interest in a process of social and political change around competing and changing values. Invariably the history of the dispute is important to the participants, with the past overshadowing the future.[1] This situation is summarised in definitions of environmental conflict, such as: "An unresolved dispute between competing interest groups which has reached the public arena, is controversial and may have political consequences. Typically one group is attempting

---

[1] HJ Brown and AL Marriott, *ADR Principles and Practice* (1993).

to control the action of others and limit their access to a natural resource."[2]

Typically there are the familiar elements that occur in many other types of conflict: the soured relationships based on emotions and misunderstandings; lack of information and arguments over the relevance; interpretation and assessment of data; mistrust based on the perceived unfairness over decision-making procedures; and competition for resources and between beliefs, ie differences over what is right or wrong or how the world should be.[3]

The scope for environmental mediation depends on identifying what is negotiable among confusion and in moving from conflict to co-operation (see Table 9.1). It may well be that relationships are embittered or that differences in beliefs predominate so as to preclude negotiation. It is vital to put history and beliefs to one side, to improve relationships over a period of time, to improve understanding of the underlying issues and to identify common goals. This is the daunting task facing environmental mediators and even when negotiations can be established the process is lengthy, taking months or even years in some cases.

TABLE 9.1   TWO SIDES OF THE SAME COIN?[4]

Conflict	Co-operation
Relationships and procedures: little direct contact between the interested parties whose approach was confrontational.	*Relationships and procedures:* frequent contact between the parties whose approach was conciliatory.
Data and understanding: uncertainty over a contentious issue with information withheld and used as form of power.	*Data and understanding:* the issue was understood or taken on trust and information shared freely.
Competing interests: goal of "winner takes all".	*Interests:* effort taken to meet all needs.
Beliefs: differences elevated to matters of non-negotiable principle.	*Beliefs:* differences respected and principles set aside.

---

[2] R Sidaway, *Resolving Environmental Disputes* (2005).
[3] D Amy, *The Politics of Environmental Mediation* (1987).
[4] R Sidaway, "Outdoor Recreation and Nature conservation: conflicts and their resolution" (unpublished Ph.D. thesis, University of Edinburgh, 1996).

THE MEDIATION PROCESS

Environmental mediation takes the form of a staged process with the initial preparatory stage of deciding whether and how to negotiate being crucial. But first someone has to take the initiative both to suggest mediation and to identify an acceptable mediator. This will probably not come from one of the principal protagonists but from an "internal advocate" who is familiar with mediation and its benefits, is not immediately involved in the conflict and is sufficiently respected and influential for the suggestion to be taken seriously.

Once a suitable mediator has been identified, she or he meets the parties individually and assesses whether there is a basis for negotiation. This preparatory stage is usually termed "conflict assessment" or "stakeholder analysis". The potential mediator sets out a strategy covering the purpose and scope of negotiation, suggests details of who should be represented, the ground rules that may be followed, a provisional timescale and whether financial resources are needed to cover the mediator's time and the collection of data on critical issues. Even more crucial is the final recommendation on whether there is a basis for negotiation at this time. Environmental mediators must have the integrity to say no; this is a key part of the ethical code that sets them apart from so many consultants. The mediator's assessment usually takes a written form which is put to the interested parties for their consideration.

If there is agreement to proceed, the mediation follows a familiar pattern. The parties exchange information without interruption (probably really listening to each other for the first time), begin to understand each other's interests, build trust, agree a common goal and explore alternative solutions. The parties gradually work towards a voluntary agreement, the form it will take and how it will be implemented. If the negotiations are successful, the agreement is ratified by the parties and its outcomes are monitored and reviewed. As in other forms of mediation, agreement on ground rules at the outset is vital. Important topics to be covered are:

- The terms of reference and the role of the mediator, particularly if the mediator is to meet individuals between formal sessions.
- The role of those participants who are representing organisations and their ability to confer between meetings of the negotiating group whilst maintaining confidentiality.
- The extent to which information is released to the media, especially when negotiations span many months.

The circumstances in which environmental mediation is likely to be effective are similar to those relating to other forms of mediation, in particular when an ongoing working relationship is important to the parties and they will accept help from an impartial third party. Often the political struggle of an environmental conflict has reached an impasse, power is more evenly balanced, there is no obvious way out of the stalemate, and there is external pressure to settle. At that point, a mediated negotiation can begin.

The balance of power is crucial in determining when mediation becomes an option during the course of an environmental dispute and whether those with the responsibility to determine the outcome will welcome more open, participatory decision-making. A reluctance to share responsibility in part may help explain why powerful government agencies have been unwilling in the past to try environmental mediation, although there is no shortage of public policy disputes.

However, the statutory planning process is an obvious candidate for the wider application of mediation, as it is seen by its critics as long-winded, costly and arguably does not resolve conflict. The opportunities to introduce mediation into the planning system are set out below.

THE BASIC STRUCTURE OF THE SCOTTISH PLANNING SYSTEM

The Scottish planning system consists of three main parts.

1. Policies to guide and promote development are set out in development plans.

2. Subsequent planning applications are judged against these policies and any other material consideration, in a process now referred to as "development management".

3. If unauthorised development takes place, or if conditions of planning consent are breached, then the planning authority may consider taking enforcement action.

Local authorities, and both National Park authorities, are the main planning authorities with responsibilities under the Planning Acts. The Scottish Government also has planning powers and responsibilities, mainly related to overseeing issues and policies of national importance and hearing appeals against planning authority decisions.

The nature of all these powers and responsibilities is being thoroughly revised following the passing of the Planning (etc) Scotland Act 2006 (hereafter the "2006 Act"). The aims of this thorough modernisation are to make the planning system more efficient and more inclusive. Since the reforms are still emerging and will not be fully in place until 2009, the present system is described here, together with an outline of likely changes.

IMPORTANCE OF COMMUNITY ENGAGEMENT

During consideration of the Planning Scotland Bill, the Scottish Parliament was anxious to build in every opportunity for community engagement in planning. The aim is to debate and resolve fundamental issues when preparing the development plan and thereby speed up the process of determining individual planning applications at a later stage. This message was reinforced in Planning Advice Note 81 (PAN 81).[5] Planning Advice Notes provide advice on good practice and other relevant information, and are mainly used by professional planners and other advisers, although all are readily available to the public.[6] PAN 81 clarifies the community engagement responsibilities of Scottish Ministers, planning authorities, councillors, applicants and their agents, community councils, voluntary, interest and amenity groups, key agencies and statutory consultees. The advice note also establishes what the community can expect from the planning process (depending on future legislation) and the standards to be met.

DEVELOPMENT PLANNING

The development plan is currently defined as the structure plan together with the local plan for an area. Seventeen structure plans, some jointly prepared by several planning authorities, cover the whole of Scotland. As part of the approval process, Scottish Ministers ensure that structure plans conform to national policy, including the National Planning Framework.

Every planning authority prepares local plans for its area. Sometimes, a single plan covers the whole area; in other instances, the area is subdivided with a separate local plan for each. In all instances, a local plan cannot be adopted (and thus become a formal part of the development plan) unless it conforms to an approved structure plan.

While local communities take a keen interest in their neighbourhoods, they appear reluctant to take an active interest in issues that seem remote and academic. Planners and politicians have long found it difficult to persuade all but the most committed to express an opinion on structure plans. So when proposals are considered in a local plan, local communities would wake up to the implications, only to find that the time to have any constructive influence had long passed. Even the best explanations can fail to abate the feelings of frustration that result. A notable example is the M74 extension in Glasgow, the

---

[5] PAN 81: *Community Engagement — Planning with People* (2007).
[6] http://www.scotland.gov.uk/Topics/Built-Environment/planning/National-Planning-Policy/themes/communities.

principle of which was debated and approved in a structure plan. It was only when compulsory purchase orders were served to assemble the land for the project that the local community began to take real notice, at which point the public local inquiry became a national *cause célèbre* as the fundamental pros and cons of urban motorways were examined in minute detail, but too late to make a difference to the policy decision.

HOW DEVELOPMENT PLANNING IS CHANGING

The 2006 Act replaces local plans with a system of local development plans which, it is hoped, will be simpler and quicker to prepare than the current generation of plans. Four strategic development plans will replace the current structure plans in the city regions centred on Glasgow, Edinburgh, Dundee and Aberdeen; elsewhere, structure plans are entirely abolished. The National Planning Framework remains, becoming a statutory responsibility of Scottish Ministers. The most significant change, however, is that all these plans will be subject to review every five years (or less). Publicity and community engagement rules are strengthened, although timetables are also tightened to avoid lengthy delays.

Given the high importance now being attached to early community engagement, it is essential that development plans gain the confidence of their communities. This will only be achieved through a sound and trustworthy engagement process early in their preparation, thorough and open monitoring of their effectiveness, and consistent application of their policies in the handling of planning applications.

OPPORTUNITIES FOR MEDIATION IN DEVELOPMENT PLANNING

Development plans take several years to prepare. They do not, however, start from an entirely blank sheet. There will already be an earlier plan in place (often well past pensionable age) and experience will have been gained of how effective its policies have been in practice. There will also be a considerable amount of information available to the planning authority on population trends, the rate of development needed and land availability. Authorities will be aware of local social and economic conditions, indicating areas in need of regeneration and of environmental issues such as areas that should be conserved or pollution hotspots.

Perhaps the most valuable information available to the planning authority will be public opinion, gathered over the years through representations made on planning applications, the views of community councils, newspaper reports, and simply through good listening. But public opinion can be fickle and unreliable, so it is difficult to tease out how opinion might change if better information were to be made available. Moreover, different groups can mistrust each other. It's not uncommon, for example, for communities to distrust major developers or, for that matter, the local council, and this lack of trust can get in the way of the dialogue necessary to resolve the underlying issues.

This is precisely the set of circumstances in which consensus building can make a difference. A skilled independent mediator should be able to ease communication between potentially opposed parties. If this can be done before the formal preparation of a plan gets under way, it will lay a much better foundation for later community engagement. It can also provide an opportunity to redirect comment in the most appropriate direction, for example, where strategic issues are at stake, towards a structure plan instead of a local plan. At the very least, the early exchange of information and views will lead to fewer nasty surprises for all parties when a proposed plan emerges.

It is interesting to speculate whether consensus building techniques could have applied to the M74 extension case mentioned earlier, and whether it would have made any difference to the final decision. What can be said with some confidence is that much of the argument would have taken place before the compulsory purchase order stage and the degree of understandable frustration in the local community may have been greatly reduced.

Once the process of preparing a plan is properly under way, a number of formal opportunities arise for the community to make its voice heard. Inevitably some issues are particularly contentious, attracting hundreds or even thousands of objections. Of course, good preparatory work and sound consensus building should allow more effort to be focused on the most important issues; but there's little doubt that a wide range of issues, involving many different parties, will remain.

Development plans can only address land use planning issues, on which there is a vast range of advice, good practice and legal precedent to consider. Inevitably, national policy and non-negotiable financial and infrastructural restrictions will also prove to be limitations. If a planning issue encounters these constraints, the scope for negotiation or mediation will be reduced.

Constrained issues aside, there are considerable opportunities for mediation to help resolve formal environmental disputes. If objections are not considered until the public inquiry, this can be a time-consuming and costly option. Yet for many objections, direct negotiation in the preliminary stages would be more appropriate and mediation can be a relatively quick way of resolving disputes. As in some other forms of mediation, an initial agreement would form the basis of a legally binding decision. Planning law dictates that any agreed outcome would then be fed into the public inquiry process, albeit in a low-key and uncontentious way. This provides formal opportunities for anyone to comment on proposed modifications to a plan.

DEVELOPMENT MANAGEMENT AND ENFORCEMENT

Planning consent is required for all forms of development which, put very simply, means a building or engineering operation, or change in the use of land. Most minor building works and many changes of use are permitted development, which can proceed without the need for a planning application. All other development requires a planning application to be lodged with the local planning authority. "Neighbouring proprietors" are notified of all applications, and some applications are also advertised in the local press or on site. Anyone may lodge an objection to any planning application, or make a representation in support. By law, a few major applications require an environmental impact assessment before they can be considered. This triggers another opportunity for public comment. The majority of straightforward planning decisions are delegated to officers of the planning authority to determine, leaving the more contentious applications to go in front of the Planning Committee. Schemes of delegation vary from authority to authority.

Planning applications must be decided in accordance with the provisions of the development plan, and any other material consideration. This underlines why communities cannot afford to ignore development plans while they are in preparation. But applications can be put forward for approval in spite of their being contrary to plan policies. There are safeguards in place to ensure that such departures are subject to extra publicity and procedures. Having considered the development plan and any other material consideration, the planning authority may approve (with or without conditions) or refuse an application.

Applicants may appeal to the Scottish Ministers against refusal of consent or the imposition of conditions. The Ministers appoint Reporters to hear these appeals, and usually delegate to them the appeal decision. Objectors have a right to take part in proceedings, which may be by written submissions, a hearing or a formal public local inquiry.

There are complicated rules governing enforcement action, which the planning authority may decide to take if development is carried out without consent or if conditions attached to consent are not implemented. The planning authority is unlikely to take enforcement action if it would have granted consent in any event. Powers available include requiring an application to be lodged, requiring certain works or action to be carried out (or even carrying it out and charging the cost to the landowner), or taking court action.

HOW DEVELOPMENT MANAGEMENT IS CHANGING

Under the 2006 Act, new classes of national and major planning applications will be created and will be subject to special treatment. National Developments in Scotland will be few and far between, such as, for example, the proposed new Firth of Forth road crossing. Major developments will probably include large housing, shopping or industrial developments. A radical new requirement will be for the promoters of such developments to enter into pre-application discussions with affected communities with the aim of informing and amending their schemes to meet community wishes. The form of community engagement will have to be agreed with the planning authority in advance and this process will be audited to ensure agreed procedures are followed. Appeals against major application decisions will have to be lodged more quickly; will be restricted more tightly to the information already lodged with the planning authority; and will less often be subject to formal public local inquiries.

Planning applications that are neither national nor major will become known as local applications. The vast majority of these will be delegated to officers to determine. Instead of an appeal process, delegated decisions are likely to be reviewed by a Review Panel made up of local councillors. Appeal to Scottish Ministers will still be available for applications determined by the planning committee in the first instance.

OPPORTUNITIES FOR MEDIATION IN DEVELOPMENT MANAGEMENT

As with development plans, the earlier in the process that negotiation takes place, the easier it will be to reach a satisfactory conclusion. The special pre-application discussions for major applications will offer a perfect opportunity for consensus building and some developers already adopt the opportunity as a matter of good practice. However, a community may be wary that a developer is not being entirely open and one possible route for countering this is to employ the services of a skilled mediator to facilitate discussions. Since major applications are bound to raise tricky issues, it is essential that the mediator should have a good knowledge of the planning system or, at the very least, should have immediate access to independent professional planning advice.

Once an application has been lodged, objections constitute a formal dispute. Provided that there is room to manoeuvre, these disputes may be amenable to mediation. An agreement at this stage cannot be the end of the matter, as only a planning authority can determine a planning application and there are many interests to consider. But most planning authorities would consider any form of agreement positively, and in any event the very process of mediation is a good way of alleviating the "winner takes all" feeling that characterises many planning disputes.

Another benefit of mediation in planning is that it allows the possibility of informal agreements being reached between a developer and objectors that go beyond the scope of planning considerations. For example, it may be that irritation over parking habits or garden maintenance could prompt someone to object to a neighbour's proposed house extension. Such matters are beyond planning's remit, but if a mediated discussion results in an amended planning application in return for other concessions, all would benefit. Similar considerations, on a larger scale, can be conceived of for major applications, although the suspicion that objectors are somehow being bought off must be guarded against. To a degree, this kind of agreement already exists in the form of benefits being offered to and accepted by communities affected by wind farms.

Finally, enforcement is an area of planning activity well suited to mediation. It is almost inevitable that there is mistrust between the planning authority and the developer, and perhaps also the surrounding community, and that normal negotiation has failed to resolve the issues in hand. In these circumstances mediation offers the possibility of willing future co-operation.

CONCLUSIONS

Environmental and planning issues are usually resolved amicably. But sometimes, bitter battles leave in their wake sore losers and bruised victors. Major developers, government agencies and local authorities can afford powerful teams of experts. The community can feel excluded if they can't muster similar resources. If you dig deeper, you may find mistrust between developers, the community and the authorities.

Mediation offers the chance to replace confrontation with negotiation. It improves understanding from the outset and builds consensus. By allowing the possibility of modifying a proposal to meet a wider range of interests, the application of mediation to planning disputes could resolve objections and speed up the approval process. But it would not replace it; final decisions remain with the relevant authorities.

Chapter 10

NEIGHBOUR/COMMUNITY MEDIATION

Ian McDonough

Modern living, whether urban, suburban or rural, is full of stress, and more and more people view their home as a place of escape or sanctuary. When this sanctuary is invaded, either by noise or other means, conflict will frequently result. Add to this the problems caused by much of modern building construction (inadequate soundproofing, poor estate design, space constraints), a sharp increase in the ownership of noisy domestic appliances, and a mobile society where people sometimes do not even know who their neighbours are, and we have an incendiary mixture which is bound to burst into flames on occasion.

This chapter describes the resolution of a typical neighbour dispute by mediators. Community mediation is a frequently used and highly successful way of assisting neighbours and groups of people in neighbourhoods resolve a wide range of conflicts. Community mediation in Scotland has grown considerably in the last ten years, and there are now services covering almost the whole of the country, from large urban conurbations to the Highlands and Islands.

CASE STUDY

The Gallaghers live on a mixed estate on the fringes of Edinburgh. Twenty-five years ago, Rainhouse Park was considered one of the more desirable council estates in the city: people could wait half a lifetime before being offered one of its three-bedroom, semi-detached houses. Following the introduction of the "right to buy" legislation, most of the properties sold quickly and now only a handful are owned by the council. Some of the purchased properties have now been rented out to private tenants and recently there has been an increase in tension between residents.

Jim Gallagher works irregular shifts as a cab driver. He was born and raised in the same house, inheriting the tenancy on his mother's death in 1989. Shortly after this he got married to Sheila and they bought the house from the council at a good discount. The Gallaghers have three children: twin boys aged 15 and a five-year old girl just about to start school. They get by, but bringing up children is expensive and Sheila works part-time at the local pub some nights if Jim's shifts allow it.

Last year the McPhails and their two sons rented the house next door to the Gallaghers from a friend. Things were tricky right from the start when they held a housewarming party that lasted until 5 am. Pretty soon it felt to the Gallaghers as though their lives had been taken over by the McPhails. There were fights between the children, late sessions every weekend and a bad-tempered argument between Sheila Gallagher and Maggie McPhail.

The tension moved up a gear when, after an all-night shift, Jim came back in a combative mood and decided to get his own back. He started to play football songs at deafening volume, waking up both his own family and the McPhails. Liam McPhail came to the Gallaghers door and asked politely if Jim could turn it down, but was told "If you don't like it, **** off back where you came from".

That afternoon Maggie and Liam reported the situation to the local police and were advised to try mediation. It didn't sound very hopeful to them. The police officer said it was voluntary and that the mediators didn't take sides, they just helped everyone to understand each other's point of view and maybe come to an agreement. He said that, funnily enough, it usually worked, so they reluctantly agreed to give it a try.

Three days later they got a phone call from the local community mediation service explaining things in more detail. The mediator sounded acceptable, so they agreed to see him and his colleague and gave their permission for the mediators to contact the Gallaghers.

At first Jim and Sheila Gallagher were furious about getting a letter from the mediation service, but when they had calmed down and actually read the letter properly, it was clear that no one was being blamed for anything. Sheila eventually persuaded Jim that they had nothing to lose by giving it a go.

The following week two mediators arrived and they explained they had already seen the McPhails but now wanted to find out what Jim and Sheila felt might be a good way forward. Jim warmed to them despite his misgivings; they were good listeners and seemed to have a practical, down-to-earth approach to things. Jim and Sheila were surprised to hear that the McPhails had agreed to a meeting with them and the mediators in the local library, and surprised themselves even more by saying they would come along too. The mediators explained that meetings like this had a very good success rate — about 80 to 90 per cent — and that it was their job as mediators to make sure everyone got the opportunity to both speak and listen and to help everyone work out what they would like to see happen in the future.

In the week leading up to the meeting, things seemed to improve of their own accord; both the McPhails and the Gallaghers kept the music low and both sets of parents sat down with their children to talk about the situation. Everyone was very apprehensive about meeting up, but reassuring phone calls from the mediators settled them a little. Jim and Liam even managed to say hello without scowling at each other.

At the mediation meeting the McPhails started off by saying what had happened from their viewpoint and what they'd like to see happen. Liam began by saying how sorry they were about the way things had turned out and admitted that the party on the first night of their tenancy had been utterly inappropriate. Maggie went on to explain that their two boys were frightened of the Gallagher twins who had been calling them names and making cut-throat signs at them. She said they were trying to make a fresh start away from their previous neighbourhood where children could not be let out to play safely but no one had minded a bit of music. Liam said he was prepared to guarantee that any weekend noise would now stop at 10 pm as they had had his cousin staying who was a "bit of a party animal" but he had just moved out.

When Jim and Sheila had their turn, they explained how their lives were really busy just struggling to make ends meet, so regular sleep was really important to them. Jim apologised for his outburst, saying it had been "well out of line" but he'd been at his wit's end. He guaranteed that any further bad behaviour from the twins would be nipped in the bud. Sheila backed him up on this, explaining that she had had no idea it was happening.

After both families had a chance to speak, the mediators opened things up for discussion. It quickly became clear that both sides had a lot in common: Liam had also been a cab driver for a while, and everyone agreed that bringing up children well was a real struggle. The mediators helped them decide acceptable noise levels and how the couples would communicate in future if problems occurred. They also offered to bring the older children together to help them get on better with each other.

At the close of the meeting everyone was relieved that so much ground had been covered and that things were back on an even keel. Jim said the meeting had made him realise how easy it was just to react without thinking and make things worse. Liam admitted he was a little ashamed of how selfish he had been. The mediators congratulated them all for dealing with the conflict so positively and agreed to contact them all in three months' time to see whether the agreement was still going well.

BACKGROUND OF COMMUNITY MEDIATION IN SCOTLAND

Not so long ago, the McPhails and Gallaghers would have had to resolve their dispute in some other way. Or if the conflict had grown unchecked, as these conflicts often do, one or more of the parties may well have ended up with a police record. It was dissatisfaction with the formal means of resolving such conflicts — treating the symptoms rather than the underlying causes — that led to the establishment of Edinburgh Community Mediation Service in 1995, which was a joint venture between SACRO and local agencies. The project quickly became championed by local community groups, police, housing officials and others, as well as being supported by the major political parties. As it established a track record for the resolution of neighbourhood conflicts across the city, the model began to be replicated in other areas, beginning with services in Dundee, Fife and Falkirk.

This process of growth was boosted by the (then) Scottish Executive which funded SACRO to establish the Community Mediation Consultancy and Training Service. This initiative was charged with assisting Scottish social housing providers in developing the provision of mediation across Scotland, to establish and promote best practice and to produce publications on all aspects of mediation in a neighbourhood context. At the same time, the Scottish Executive introduced a funding stream (Building Safer, Stronger Communities) which further assisted local authorities in financing neighbourhood mediation; by 2007 30 of the 32 Scottish local authority areas had mediation services, managed in-house, by SACRO, or in one case by a local voluntary organisation.

Community mediation is now a widespread and well-established tool for dispute resolution in Scotland, with thousands of neighbour disputes having been handled by mediators. Most cases involve two sets of neighbours, but some involving whole neighbourhoods of 50 to 100 or more households. All the services are listed by location on the Scottish Mediation Network website under "Find a Mediator".

Community mediation has its own accreditation scheme developed by the umbrella body, the Scottish Community Mediation Network, and mediation is built into many local authority procedures. Services will differ in the detail of their practice but the majority will take referrals from local police, housing departments, environmental services and a range of other agencies, as well as from people directly involved in disputes themselves.

Mediation services usually only need one party in the dispute to agree to try mediation. It is part of the mediator's job to help the other party agree to participate: something they generally manage very successfully. Mediators meet both of the parties, usually in their homes, and explain what mediation involves. They will listen to their description of the dispute, including its origins, the current situation, how they feel about it, what they would like to see happen, and whether they would be prepared to meet the other neighbour in a mediation meeting. Some disputes are settled at this point, without proceeding to a mediation meeting, through a simple process of talking over options and giving advice to people on how to manage the conflict themselves. In many other disputes, however, the conflict has reached a stage where only the full mediation process will resolve it.

TRENDS IN COMMUNITY MEDIATION

A recent notable trend in community mediation in Scotland has been the willingness of services to widen their area of involvement. Although individual neighbour disputes remain the major area of activity, many services now provide mediation for young people threatened with homelessness and their families, mediation in a workplace context, mediation between organisations, and a wide range of school-based work.

Large group mediations in particular are becoming increasingly frequent. Community mediators now regularly handle conflicts which are affecting groups in the community; these range from issues between several residents in a tenement stair, disputes affecting a whole street, or situations which are district-wide and involve a hundred or more people.

This last development is likely to be of particular relevance to the future direction of community mediation in Scotland. As a tool for intervention in situations of individual conflict, mediation uncovers practical solutions, demonstrates more positive forms of communication, reframes contentious issues into shared problems, and often gives disputants a different perspective on the actions of themselves and their immediate neighbours. This in itself will have an impact on the general well-being of communities. Fewer individual conflicts means more energy is available for other things since people who are under the immediate pressure of such conflicts are often unlikely to be able to look further than their own back fence.

In recent years, however, Scottish community mediation services have increasingly realised that individual casework is only a part of the answer to the incidence of destructive conflict in Scottish communities. For people with little power or status, living in poverty and in poor housing conditions, the problem with their neighbour may be low on their list of priorities: something on which they can afford to expend only limited energy. Some critics of mediation have taken this argument further, by accusing it of shoring up injustice by a tacit acceptance of the power imbalances inherent in society. In this argument, community mediation is seen as encouraging deprived groups to accept situations which should not be tolerated. In the case of council tenants on an estate where the soundproofing is completely inadequate, such critics would argue that to assist neighbours to come to agreement about their respective levels of living noise is not only failing to identify and deal with the real problem, but is hindering any effective action by focussing the issue on the behaviour of the individuals rather than the responsibilities of the landlord. In other words, as long as mediation focuses exclusively on individual issues, it cannot be said to be assisting in the development of strong, positive and equitable communities.

But how far should community mediators assist in the development of strong, positive and equitable communities? Mediation is sometimes viewed as a completely neutral process, unaffected by either the beliefs of the mediator or those held by the disputants. Moreover, it is often further claimed to have no interest in or views on the agreements reached and the situations of people in conflict. Indeed some mediators hold that any general consideration of the justice or injustice, equity or inequity of groups in the community is no concern of theirs.

This "neutral" and "individualised" model of conflict resolution is, however, being challenged. Most Scottish community mediation services are increasingly arguing that in order to deal with the roots of neighbourhood issues, the conflicts between larger groups in communities need to be resolved as constructively as possible, and that mediation is able to ensure disadvantaged groups have a voice. These mediation services view community mediation as growing into a key component in broader concerns of community development, and an option of first choice in helping the most challenged communities turn themselves around by working together to make their views heard effectively. The challenge ahead for community mediators in Scotland may be to contribute meaningfully to the strengthening and development of disadvantaged groups and communities while retaining their impartial role in the resolution of individual conflicts.

Chapter 11

FAMILY MEDIATION

Rosanne Cubitt

Family mediation helps families in conflict to work through their difficulties and to agree on a way forward that supports improved family communication; it helps families to make their own decisions about the future. Family mediators can work directly with children to ensure their voice is heard and included in the mediation process.

Family mediation can work in parallel with negotiations through lawyers and court action, and it can help to avoid lengthy, potentially acrimonious, legal battles. Family mediators in Scotland are trained to a high standard and are accredited by professional bodies. They work to a code of practice which ensures adherence to the principles of mediation.

CASE STUDY 1

Jane and Ross decide to separate after 15 years of married life. They have two children: Stacy who is 11, and Ashley who is eight. There have been heated arguments between Jane and Ross over the last few years, resulting in their drifting further and further apart. They struggle to communicate with one another in a civil way and have both been for relationship counselling. It is clear now that their relationship is over. Jane wants Ross to move out so that she can get on with her life. Ross is reluctant to leave the family home as he wants to make sure he can still see his children regularly. There are financial issues to resolve and Ross and Jane are not sure how they can set up two homes for the children. Both are keen to minimise the disruption for their children but cannot talk about anything as verbal exchanges become a hurtful round of accusation and counter-accusation.

Jane's solicitor suggests that they might want to consider family mediation as a way of working through some of their difficulties.

Jane contacts the local family mediation service and makes an appointment to find out more. She talks through her concerns and is given information about the mediation process and other services that are available. Ross agrees to give mediation a try, and he too has an initial, one-to-one meeting at the family mediation service. Having found out more, it seems that maybe mediation might help. Jane and Ross participate in three joint mediation sessions, each lasting for about an hour. Through these sessions they are able to talk about their concerns, issues and fears. The mediator encourages them to see things from different perspectives, helping them realise that they both want the same thing: a good, lasting relationship with each of their children. They realise that they need to work together if they are going to achieve this.

An agreement is reached whereby Ross will move in with his parents (the children being able to stay with him there), while Jane and Ross work towards the sale of the family home and the purchase of two smaller houses. They agree that the girls will continue to live in the family home in the short term, and that they will spend every other weekend with Ross, as well as every Wednesday night. The girls will go straight to their grandmother's house after school on a Wednesday and Ross will be able to drop them at school on his way to work in the morning. Jane and Ross agree that they will communicate any changes to these arrangements by mobile phone. They agree that the children can call the parent that they are not staying with whenever they like.

After the three mediation sessions, Jane and Ross feel that they are communicating well enough to be able to agree the organisation of the summer holidays that are still some months away. They agree to contact the service again if they are unable to sort this out themselves, or if issues arise again in the future. The introduction of a new partner to the children is perceived as a potential future issue by both Jane and Ross, but is not an imminent concern.

CASE STUDY 2

Katie is 16 and has been living on her own with her Mum since her Mum, Aileen, and Dad, Colin, separated six years ago. She sees her Dad occasionally but he has moved away from town since getting a new job and his visits back are becoming less and less frequent. Katie has recently got in with a new group of friends and is spending more and more time out with them in the evenings, getting home very late at night.

Aileen is not happy with the way Katie's social life is developing, nor is she happy with her attitude and her unwillingness to talk about what she and her friends do when they are out. Aileen suspects that the friends Katie is getting involved with are taking drugs and drinking too much. The situation comes to a head when Katie does not come home at all one Saturday night, does not call to say where she is, and is very rude to her Mum when she finally does come home. There is a blazing row between them. Katie accuses her Mum of not really caring about her, saying that if she did, she would not have split up with her Dad. Katie threatens to leave home and find somewhere to live on her own, where she will not be harassed about how she spends her time. She says that as she is 16 now, her Mum cannot make her stay any more. Aileen is devastated with this turn of events.

Aileen and Colin went to family mediation following their decision to separate so Aileen approaches the service to find out whether she and Katie can now meet with someone, to help them talk through their concerns without the arguments getting out of hand. Katie is initially very resistant to the idea. She thinks to herself "What will some random adult remember about life as a teenager? And anyway, they will be bound to side with Mum". Deep down, Katie does not really want to leave home. She is actually scared about the idea, but does want her Mum to get off her back and let her do what she wants, when she wants. She loves her Mum but resents the fact that she and her Dad have separated.

Katie decides to give mediation a try, although she does not hold out much hope. She meets with the mediator initially on her own and is able to talk about how she feels. The mediator is really good at listening and seems interested in her situation. Katie feels the mediator understands and does not preach about how teenagers should behave. The mediator says each family has to work it out for themselves.

One week on, Katie and Aileen both meet with the mediator. They are each asked to put forward the issues as they see them. Katie feels able to say what she thinks because the mediator seems to respect her views and sometimes asks her Mum not to interrupt but to let Katie speak for herself. Aileen realises that Katie has needed the chance to speak and to be heard without feeling judged. After two joint meetings Katie and Aileen are able to agree some boundaries for going out at night which they both think are reasonable. Katie has been able to tell her Mum more about her friends, and Aileen agrees to trust her to behave appropriately and safely when she is out. There is no further discussion about Katie moving out of the family home.

FAMILY MEDIATION IN CONTEXT

Mediation in the family context has a long established history. It emerged in Scotland in the early 1980s to help parents who were divorcing or separating to agree on arrangements for the future parenting of their children. It can work in parallel with negotiations through lawyers and court action. Frequently it offers an alternative to the court process, and the often acrimonious legal disputes that have the potential to drive families further apart.

The focus of family mediation is on the needs of the parties and any children caught up in family disputes. When two people decide to separate, the ensuing emotional upheaval sometimes makes it difficult to keep the focus on the children and to put their needs first. Family mediators help to address this by working with parents to facilitate their communication and to encourage them to think about the needs of their children. Typically, family mediation focuses on:

- where the children will live following separation;
- when and where the children will see their parents through the week;
- how they will spend holidays and special days;
- how parents will handle any health and education matters;
- how they want to communicate as a family in the future.

Family mediation can also help separating partners to agree on a way forward with financial and property issues arising from divorce or separation.

Some family mediators work with partners who are separating but do not have children. Family mediation can also be an appropriate and helpful resource for resolving conflict in other aspects of family life. Increasingly, family mediators are meeting with grandparents, step-parents, siblings and other family members to work through a wide range of issues that arise in the course of family life.

There is not one best solution that suits everyone, as every family is unique and has to work around different practical constraints. Mediation can help to minimise the potentially negative impact of divorce or separation on children, improving the chances of these children reaching their full potential. It can also be a crucial step in the prevention of teenage homelessness.

RESOURCES

In Scotland, family mediation is available through a network of local family mediation services affiliated to Relationships Scotland, and from a number of family lawyers who have also been trained to work as mediators, called CALM mediators. Family mediation is also offered by independent mediators.

The Relationships Scotland affiliated services are not-for-profit, charitable organisations and are funded through a range of grants, including financial support from the Scottish Government. Clients can participate in child-focused mediation at no cost to them. There is normally a small charge for mediation on financial and property matters. These services offer a range of other family support services, such as child contact centres, children and parents' support groups, and counselling, some of which may incur a nominal charge.

A CALM mediator's role is different from that of a solicitor. The aim of a family mediator who has a background as a lawyer is to help to clarify the questions that need to be settled and to explore the available options. CALM mediators can provide legal information in an impartial way and can explain how any proposed settlement terms can be made legally binding. CALM mediators charge a fee that is normally discussed before mediation begins. Clients who are eligible for Legal Aid can apply through their lawyer for their share of the cost of the mediation to be covered. CALM family mediators tend to work with parties who also have financial issues to sort out. Finances can include houses, pensions, savings and maintenance.

Independent family mediators can assist with a wide range of issues that face families in times of conflict. Freelance mediators also charge a fee which should be discussed before mediation begins. Independent family mediators often are willing to travel and are excellent resources if there is not a local family mediation service available nearby.

Most clients interested in finding out more about the services of family mediation make contact with the organisations directly themselves. Clients may also be referred to mediation by the courts, solicitors, health care professionals, social workers, counselling services, Citizens Advice Bureaux, and other similar organisations.

All family mediators are trained to a very high standard and are generally accredited either through Relationships Scotland or through the Law Society of Scotland (CALM mediators). Information about independent family mediators can be found on the Scottish Mediation Register website. In addition to generic mediation skills training, family mediators are also trained to develop an in-depth understanding of family specific issues such as child development and children's needs, family systems, child protection, domestic abuse, the impact of separation and loss, as well as the context of family law.

THE FAMILY MEDIATION PROCESS

In most cases, once contact has been established, clients will be invited to attend individually an initial meeting or to speak to a mediator on the phone. During this one-to-one discussion, the family member will often be encouraged to explain their situation and the family issues or areas of conflict that they are struggling with. Following an explanation of the mediation process and its underlying principles, the mediator, together with the client, will establish whether mediation is the next appropriate step.

Once all parties to the dispute have had this initial discussion, and if the decision is taken to go ahead with mediation, they will be invited to a joint meeting with a mediator. Generally, the mediator will meet with the parties for three or four sessions over a period of weeks. There is flexibility around this timetable to accommodate specific circumstances. The meetings can take place at a variety of venues including the premises of the mediation service provider, or other community venues such as family centres. It is possible for clients to return to mediation again at a later stage if their circumstances change and they feel that mediation would help them.

During mediation the participants often realise that they have common goals, such as the desire to improve relationships within the family and to improve the quality of life for the children. It is important for separating parents, in particular, to recognise that their co-parenting role in the future is critical to their children realising their potential and feeling safe, secure and loved. Parents are the experts on their children's lives and are generally better placed to make the decisions about their future than solicitors or the courts.

IMPORTANT TO KNOW

Disputes within families are different from many other types of disputes in that there is generally a desire to have on-going relationships with other family members. This can provide the motivation to work to overcome difficulties. This is particularly the case for separating parents whose own adult relationship may be over, but who remain mum and dad to their children for life. There is a strong imperative to work towards effective future communication for the sake of the children.

Confidentiality in family mediation is a key principle. It allows parties to speak openly about their issues and concerns in the knowledge that discussions within family mediation stay within the mediation sessions. The only exceptions to this are if concerns are raised about safety, particularly of children, or of criminal activities. The Civil Evidence (Family Mediation) (Scotland) Act 1995 supports this principle and establishes that what occurs during family mediation sessions cannot be used in civil legal proceedings, unless both parties agree or if issues regarding children's safety present themselves. If child safety issues arise mediation will usually be suspended.

Both the Children (Scotland) Act 1995 and the Family Law (Scotland) Act 2006 are based on the underlying principle that the welfare of the child is to be the paramount consideration. Older children (usually aged 12 years or over) are to be given the opportunity to express their views before the courts make decisions regarding their welfare.

The same is true of family mediation. If appropriate, family mediators will meet with children and young people individually, to offer them the chance to express their thoughts and feelings regarding any arrangements that their parents or family members are considering. Family mediation gives children and young people a voice and ensures that their needs are the focus of decisions that are being made about them. It is often assumed that children do not know what is best for them, but actually children often have good ideas and suggestions to make. Sometimes the adults are the ones who lose perspective.

When working with young people, the role of the mediator is to take agreed feedback to the parents, and to ensure that the children's views are included in the mediation process. Family mediators are trained specifically to offer this service. For this process to be effective and supportive for children, the parents have to be prepared to take into consideration their children's views.

Family mediators work hard to be impartial and even-handed in the way they manage the mediation process. They do not take sides with either party. This means they are alert to power differences and will work towards redressing significant imbalances. In families where domestic abuse is an issue, additional safeguards are put in place. In such instances it may not be appropriate for the parties to mediate their issues until a later stage.

CONCLUSION

Mediating with families in dispute is important because of the long-term effects of family breakdown. When family members respect and value one another, regardless of whether parents have separated or not, the results are beneficial not only to the individuals themselves but also to society at large. Conversely, in families where communication has broken down or is under significant strain, the negative consequences can be far reaching. At least one in three children in the UK is affected by parental separation before the age of 16.[1] It is estimated that family conflict is the main cause of

---

[1] M Maclean, "Together and Apart — Children and Parents Experiencing Separation and Divorce", *Foundations* (Joseph Rowntree Foundation, 2004), Ref 314.

homelessness for at least two-thirds and possibly up to 90 per cent of homeless young people.[2] The task of a family mediator is to improve the outcomes for families by improving communication, reducing conflict, and supporting relationships within the family.

Through mediation both parties in a conflict have the opportunity to overcome their difficulties without the intervention of statutory agencies or the courts. Mediation can be used very effectively to avoid lengthy legal battles or acrimonious correspondence. Agreements are more likely to last because the parties have worked through the issues and developed solutions for themselves. When people learn to communicate more effectively with one another they are better placed to make new agreements as the needs of their family change over time. As a result, society achieves long-term positive benefits and savings are made to the public purse.

---

[2] G Randall and S Brown, "Trouble at Home: Family Conflict, Young People and Homelessness" (2001), p 13.

Chapter 12

RIGHTS-BASED CONCILIATION/DISABILITY CONCILIATION

Morag Steven

The Disability Conciliation Service (DCS) operates throughout the UK and Northern Ireland. It provides an opportunity to resolve complaints relating to the Disability Discrimination Act 1995 (DDA) as an alternative to legal action through the courts. The DDA is UK-wide legislation. In March 2001 the DCS began work to deal with issues relating to goods, facilities and services which involve the vast majority of organisations providing a service to the public. Examples of services are going to a restaurant, shopping for clothes or food, using the local library, going to church or visiting a solicitor or doctor.

In September 2003, the DCS also began to deal with issues relating to education. Examples of educational issues are: the reasonable adjustments needed for study by a pupil or student such as visual aids, adjustments to computer software, or more time for examinations. Other types of alleged discrimination are currently not dealt with by the DCS.

What is the difference between conciliation and mediation? For many people, the answer to this question is nothing at all. However, on examination there are some small yet distinctive differences between mediation and the conciliation process offered by the DCS. For example, in mediation the parties are encouraged to have their say and listen to each other in an equitable way where no one's point of view is more important than another's. In a DCS conciliation meeting however, there is a presumption that the Disability Discrimination Act has been breached and that amends will have to be made. Even the language is different: in mediation those involved are referred to as "parties" but in DCS conciliation there is a "complainant" and a "respondent".

CASE STUDY 1

Maureen, a disabled woman with a physical impairment, visited a fish and chip shop, accompanied by her daughter. Maureen's disability meant that she was unable to take the stairs to the upstairs restaurant. They requested the same service as other customers (eating from plates and being able to order tea etc) on a table located in the downstairs takeaway section of the shop. The staff offered to carry the woman up the stairs but this was refused on health and safety grounds. As a result they had to eat standing up in the takeaway area. The only adjustment made was the provision of proper knives and forks.

Full and final settlement was reached through conciliation. The fish and chip shop agreed to provide an identical service to that offered in the restaurant to anyone unable to use the stairs to the upstairs restaurant, with immediate effect. It was agreed that a sign would be displayed, informing customers that an identical service was available downstairs if they were unable to climb the stairs to the restaurant. The restaurant agreed to write a letter of apology.

CASE STUDY 2

Mrs Aitken, who has a visual impairment, had previously received her credit card statements in Braille for the past six years. However, for the past five months she had not received any statements at all.

By the end of the conciliation meeting, full and final settlement was reached. Ms Jones, a representative from the credit card company, agreed to look at Mrs Aitken's account and the cycle date and would send Mrs Aitken a calendar transcribed into Braille so that she would know when her statements would be produced. Ms Jones would speak to Mrs Aitken regarding the issues of abbreviations and the binding of the statements produced. Ms Jones would ensure that the back office team in the customer services centre (who deal with the provision of alternative format statements) would check accounts on a daily basis and send for transcriptions on the same day. This would result in a three-working-day delay between the printed statement and the Braille statement being sent out. The company was in the process of investigating how it would set up an automated way of doing this and disability awareness training would be given to all permanent contact centre staff as part of their induction. Ms Jones and Mrs Aitken exchanged telephone numbers and agreed to liaise on a regular basis regarding outstanding issues. Compensation of £600 was agreed.

REFERRAL TO THE DCS

Until very recently, all referrals to the DCS came from the Disability Rights Commission. However, on 1 October 2007 the Disability Rights Commission was merged together with the Equal Opportunities Commission and the Commission for Racial Equality into one single Commission, the Equality and Human Rights Commission (EHRC). The EHRC is a non-departmental public body established under the Equality Act 2006, accountable for its public funds, but independent of government. The new commission not only brings together the work of these three previous equality commissions, but also takes on responsibility for the other aspects of equality: age, sexual orientation and religion or belief, as well as human rights.

In the first instance, disabled people who feel they may have been discriminated against should contact the EHRC to lodge their complaint.[1] The helpline can provide further information about conciliation and discuss whether the process may be appropriate in a particular case. In every case there must be an alleged breach of the Disability Discrimination Act relating to goods, facilities and services (Pt III of the Act)[2] or education (Pt IV).[3] In Scotland, complaints can be considered for referral where a disabled person is aged 12 or over.

The Equality and Human Rights Commission must first make sure that there is a legal basis for the complaint and that conciliation is the best way forward. Several factors can influence whether an individual is able to access the Disability Conciliation Service including whether the disabled person satisfies the DDA definition of disability, when the incident took place, the age of the disabled person and whether conciliation appears to be the best way forward. Only if both the Complainant and Respondent agree to take part in conciliation will the case be referred to the DCS.

TIMESCALES

When a disabled person alleges that they have been discriminated against, under the DDA they have six months from the date of the incident during which to lodge a case in court. If both parties agree to use conciliation, a further two months is added to the time period. The extra time means that if conciliation does not resolve the matter or if either party pulls out of the conciliation process, the disabled person still has time to consider taking the

---

[1] See Appendix 2 for contact details.
[2] http://www.opsi.gov.uk/acts/acts1995/ukpga_19950050_en_4#pt3.
[3] http://www.opsi.gov.uk/acts/acts1995/ukpga_19950050_en_5#pt4.

case through the court. This means that conciliation is an ideal "first resort". There are no disadvantages to either party and the potential benefits are enormous.

THE CONCILIATION PROCESS

Once both parties have agreed to conciliation, the DCS works intensively with each one to prepare for the conciliation meeting. This preparation work is mainly done by telephone. It is important that everyone understands the conciliation process and the significance of the Disability Discrimination Act. The disabled person (the complainant) is encouraged to identify what they would like to talk about at the conciliation meeting, and a list of their desired agreements is drawn up in writing; this forms the agenda for the meeting. A typical agenda could include:

- discussion of the incident, in light of the DDA;
- options to make reasonable adjustments;
- apology;
- DDA awareness training for staff;
- compensation and/or expenses incurred. (Under the DDA, financial compensation is not available in school cases.)

At the same time, preparation takes place with the service provider (the respondent) to make sure they are well informed about the DDA, about service providers' duties under the DDA, and that they feel ready for the meeting. The complainant's list of desired agreements is also shared with the respondent in advance of the meeting.

The conciliation meeting is an opportunity for the parties to come together and find their own solutions to the difficulties and alleged breach of the DDA, with the help of the conciliator, to avoid going to court. Meetings can last from one hour to over five hours, depending on the complexity of the case. Only in very exceptional cases would a further meeting be considered.

The conciliator's role at the meeting is to manage and focus the meeting towards a resolution. They can provide information and clarification about the DDA and service providers' duties. Within the conciliation process the rights of disabled people are a non-negotiable issue. The conciliator is active in ensuring that the disabled person's issues are addressed and in suggesting ways in which the service or education provider might meet their obligations. The conciliator will also be clear as to whether a proposed solution would uphold the disabled person's rights. At the end of the meeting the complainant is asked whether the agreements reached represent a "full and final settlement" of their claim under the DDA. If so, they commit to taking no further action against the respondent. If they choose "no settlement" they keep their option to pursue the matter in court. Therefore, in this conciliation model there is no opportunity for part agreement: there is only full agreement or no agreement.

The Conciliation Outcome Form is signed by both the complainant and the respondent and it becomes a legally binding document. Because the DCS is an independent and confidential service, no information about any conciliation case is shared without the agreement of both parties. The only information that is always shared with EHRC is whether or not full and final settlement was reached. However, parties are asked to indicate in writing if they would agree to a copy of any agreements reached being shared with Equality and Human Rights Commission. They are also asked if they are willing to be contacted by EHRC to discuss using details of their case for publicity and training purposes. None of this information is shared outwith DCS unless both parties give their permission.

BENEFITS OF USING CONCILIATION

Ultimately, disabled people who believe that they may have been discriminated against may take their case to a court of law but this may be a costly, time-consuming and confrontational process. Conciliation provides an alternative approach to resolving disputes achieving in the process settlements that lead to lasting change for disabled people and not simply compensatory payments.

Some of the benefits of conciliation are that:

- It is free of charge to both parties: there are no court fees to consider.
- It can take less time than going to court: complaints using disability conciliation usually progress to a meeting within eight weeks of being referred by the DRC.
- It is a confidential process: information about discussions which took place during the process would not be admissible in any subsequent court action.
- A negotiated outcome is more likely to be satisfactory to both parties.
- Businesses and organisations which are willing to reach a negotiated settlement are likely to be viewed more favourably by potential service and education users, particularly disabled people.

- It is empowering for the disabled person and can achieve a wide range of outcomes, such as an apology, an explanation, compensation or a commitment from the service or education provider to change policies or procedures.
- It can lead to real social change: service or education providers who engage in conciliation are able to learn about disabled people and their rights and the process can encourage them to make lasting changes voluntarily.

CONCILIATION AND ACCESSIBILITY

The Disability Conciliation Service works extremely hard to meet everyone's needs in relation to accessibility. Disabled people are asked what they need and the DCS corresponds and interacts with them according to their individual needs. The conciliation process itself is flexible enough to be adapted to any circumstance. Meetings are always arranged as close to the disabled person's home as possible and venues are chosen to be neutral and also accessible to those using them. British Sign Language interpreters, lip speakers and palantypists can be provided so that everyone can participate fully in a face-to-face meeting. The service will also work with advocates/ supporters where appropriate. In a small number of situations a face-to-face meeting is not possible or appropriate. In these cases the conciliation process can take place by telephone conferencing, e-mail or fax.

FEEDBACK FROM SERVICE USERS[4]

"Thank you! The service was exemplary and helped us reach a settlement with relative ease. I was absolutely dreading the meeting and was anxious and very apprehensive. I shouldn't have been as I was well prepared. I only wish I had been brave enough to take action sooner. I have learnt a great deal from the whole process, which will enable me to manage situations better in the future." (Complainant)

"I wouldn't have been able to solve my problem without the DCS. Phone conferencing was essential to allow me to access conciliation." (Complainant)

"A very valuable service. I believe I gained a great deal more in terms of knowledge and experience than I would have, had the case gone to court. Thank you." (Respondent)

---

[4] Excerpts from "A Pathway to Success" (Disability Conciliation Service, 2004).

LEGAL DEFINITIONS

Disability discrimination

The Disability Discrimination Act makes it unlawful for disabled people to be discriminated against in:

- employment;
- trade organisations and qualifications bodies;
- access to goods, facilities and services;
- the management, buying or renting of land or property education.

The DDA has been amended and extended several times since 1995, with a view to ending the discrimination faced by many disabled people in their everyday lives.

Definition of "disability"

The Disability Discrimination Act says that a disabled person is someone with "a physical or mental impairment which has a sub-stantial and long-term adverse effect on his ability to carry out normal day-to-day activities".[5]

Examples include cancer, diabetes, multiple sclerosis and heart conditions; hearing or sight impairments, or a significant mobility difficulty; and mental health conditions or learning difficulties. People in these circumstances and some others (such as people with a facial disfigurement) are likely to have rights under the DDA to protect them from discrimination. However, only the courts can say whether a particular individual is defined as disabled under the legislation.

---

[5] Disability Discrimination Act 1995, Pt 1, s 1(1).

Chapter 13

PEER MEDIATION IN SCHOOLS

Carol Hope

Peer mediation involves school students acting as impartial third parties to help their peers resolve conflicts, such as name-calling, bullying, arguing and fighting. The pupil mediators facilitate communication and conflict resolution. They work with their peers to find solutions where both parties feel that the outcome of the agreement reached is fair. Peer mediation is a service provided by pupils for pupils. It enables young people to resolve conflicts within the school and develop communication skills. Peer mediation is effective in all levels of schooling: primary, secondary and university levels.

Peer mediation is a voluntary process and the mediators work in pairs. Peer mediation helps pupils develop new skills like team work, critical thinking, problem-solving and negotiation skills. Helping children develop emotional intelligence and problem-solving skills results in increased confidence and self-esteem. Many teachers tell mediation trainers that they feel children have lost the capacity to solve problems, as, at all times children are surrounded by adults, even when they play outside in the playground. Peer mediation training gives children the opportunity to learn new skills and hone their existing skills.

Peer mediation trainers often talk about the "added value" that peer mediation training provides. If the school adopts a "whole school" approach to peer mediation and conflict resolution and sees the provision of mediation as an investment, then peer mediation can help to change the culture in schools. Schools and teachers benefit from:

- improved behaviour and attendance;
- improved relationships;
- a more inclusive, calm and caring environment;

- more teaching time, as teachers' time is less often taken up by resolving disputes between pupils;
- the creation of listening and democratic schools;
- reductions in conflict, therefore increases in the capacity for learning.

As with other types of mediation, peer mediation practice is continually developing and although it is too early to predict if one style is more popular than the other or if other styles will emerge, the two favoured styles at the moment are transformative and problem-solving mediation. The first case study looks at problem-solving peer mediation and the second case study looks at transformative peer mediation.

CAST STUDY 1: PROBLEM-SOLVING APPROACH

John and Robert were best friends and both families had gone on camping trips together. The two boys have had a fall-out after one of them was chosen to play football for the school team.

John was upset and angry because he thought he was a better player and was mad with Robert because he got picked to play; John thought Robert was rubbish. Robert was angry and annoyed with John because he had heard from other boys that John was telling everyone that Robert was a rubbish footballer and had only got picked because his Dad was on the school board. Both boys had started to take odd days off school with tummy pains and sore heads. The guidance teacher suggested they try mediation to resolve the conflict between them.

The peer mediators take the boys through the five stages of mediation as explained later in the chapter. They are given the opportunity to tell their side of the story and to hear how each other feels. Neither Robert nor John had realised that this situation was making them both so unhappy. The mediators help the boys look at how this conflict has been impacting on their daily life. The boys talk about not eating and finding it hard to sleep. They also work out that they had no control over the decision to pick the football team and that is nothing to do with Robert's Dad. The mediators help them explore options.

John agrees to stop telling every one that Robert was a rubbish footballer and admitted that he said this because he was jealous of Robert. Robert agrees to ask the team coach if John could help out with the football team in some way. They both said they missed each other and agreed to be friends again.

CASE STUDY 2: TRANSFORMATIVE APPROACH

Transformative peer mediators view conflict as being about relationships. Instead of focusing on individual interests and needs, transformative mediators see conflict as a "crisis of deterioration in human interaction".[1] Conflict is a sudden change in the way people usually — and preferably — relate to each other. What affects people most about conflict is the way it leads them to behave and feel.

John and Lucy are fourth-year pupils who have had an argument about whose turn it is to use the class computer. The teacher refers them to mediation. As always, there is more to this story: John wants to use the computer so that he can complete his assignment on time because he needs to achieve good exam results. Lucy wants to use the computer because she has been working hard all morning and needs to take a break.

The transformative peer mediators ask John and Lucy to explain fully the impact the conflict has had on them. They hear that John had a good relationship with Lucy but this incident caused him to snap at her and lose his temper. John told the mediators that this was not what he intended and that he was upset because he didn't normally act in this way. Lucy told the mediators that she was embarrassed as this happened in front of the whole class and she didn't know how to handle John's hostility towards her. The mediators gave John and Lucy the opportunity to talk about these feelings.

Lucy and John agreed that their relationship was more important than the conflict over the use of the school computer and had each underestimated the value of that friendship. Talking about their feelings with the help of trained mediators helped them to identify this.

By focusing on the relationship, transformative peer mediators allowed the conflict experience and the mediation to belong to the parties. When the agreement was reached, what was important was that it had meaning to both Lucy and John.

TRANSFORMATIVE AND PROBLEM-SOLVING MEDIATION

Transformative mediators believe that people seek out mediation because the experience of conflict can be negative and alienating. Transformative mediators help by supporting the parties' efforts to change their negative experience of conflict into one that is positive,

---

[1] R A B Bush, and J P Folger, *The Promise of Mediation* (2nd edn, 2005), p 46.

or at least neutral. Transformative mediators do not look to control the process or the outcome of the mediation. The parties decide what happens, how it happens, where it goes, and when it ends. The mediator's role is to help bring closure to the conflict experience, so that the people involved can get past it and move on.

Problem-solving mediators tend to start from the point that people in a conflict want a mediator to provide a procedure that is likely to lead to an acceptable solution. Accordingly, problem-solving mediators often refer to their role as "controlling the process" of the mediation, while the parties control the outcome.

With problem-solving peer mediation, mediators help by leading the parties through a multi-step negotiation procedure. The peer mediator "listens to both sides and helps the disputants move effectively through each step of the problem-solving negotiation sequence".[2] If the negotiation is successful, it will produce an agreement that both parties believe is "fair, just, and workable".[3]

PEER MEDIATION AND BULLYING

Peer mediation is not a quick and simple answer to all bullying problems. It is one strategy that can be utilised to address bullying but for it to be successful, there are a number of factors and strategies that must support and complement this method. An organisational culture in schools that encourages respect, values opinions, celebrates differences and promotes positive relationships will make it all the more difficult for bullying behaviour to flourish or be tolerated. The overarching ethos of any school should make it clear that bullying is never acceptable and that all adults and children and young people understand the role that they play in addressing bullying. Peer mediation is one aspect of supporting this culture.

HOW PEER MEDIATION WORKS

Typically, a primary or secondary school will have a peer mediation service operating over lunch time two or three times each week. During this time, two of the team of usually 20 trained peer mediators will be on duty to provide mediation, if required. A pupil can approach the mediators when they have fallen out with someone or have been involved in a fight with another pupil and ask for mediation.

The mediator will then approach the other person involved and ask if they are willing to come to mediation to try to resolve the dispute.

---

[2] D W Johnson, and R T Johnson, *Teaching Students to be Peacemakers* (3rd edn, 2005), pp 1–5.
[3] Johnson and Johnson, pp 1–5.

They then go straight into mediation. The mediators introduce themselves, explain the ground rules for mediation and explain that mediation is confidential, that mediators don't takes sides and that they don't offer solutions.

Some schools have a "worry box" or referral system. Pupils fill in a simple form stating what the problem is and who they have the problem with or they write on a piece of paper what the problem is or that they would like to speak with a mediator about the possibility of mediation. The mediators then have an individual session with the person with the problem and then invite the other pupil for an individual session to talk about the issues and the possibility of mediation. Seeing both pupils individually gives the mediators the opportunity to have face-to-face time with both pupils before the mediation session to explore the issues, to explain the role of the mediator and how mediation works.

Most peer mediators have been trained in a four- or five-step staged approach to helping the parties in conflict to resolve the dispute.

- The first stage is a welcome from the mediators and introduction to the ground rules of mediation.
- The second stage is finding out both sides of the story.
- The third stage is what they think now they have heard the other person's side of the story and finding out a bit more about how this situation is making them both feel.
- The fourth stage is helping the parties explore options.
- The fifth stage is reaching agreement (or not).

As peer mediation continues to grow and develop, more people are also discussing the possibility of introducing the transformative mediation approach, as illustrated in Case Study 2.

THE "WHOLE SCHOOL" APPROACH

This approach works on the premise that in order to make peer mediation effective, the whole school needs to address the issue of how conflict is managed. The school needs to start with a self-audit. An audit asks questions such as:

- How are conflicts managed?
- How big a problem is conflict in the school?
- What kind of conflicts does it have?
- Are the problems schoolroom based or playground based or do they come from outside influences?

The school usually needs to form a working group to take peer mediation forward. The approach usually involves all staff in the school, from head teacher to janitor. It is also important to involve all classes and parents too. Many peer mediation trainers believe that it is crucial to the success and sustainability of peer mediation to have a whole school approach.

THE "WHOLE COMMUNITY" APPROACH

In some areas of Scotland, people are looking at the provision of a peer mediation service in schools as part of a peace-making process. This approach looks at the wider cultures within communities and in some areas, street workers and community education staff are looking at developing a mediation approach to managing conflict. It encourages the use of mediation as a way to resolve conflict not just in school but recognises that by the time a young person leaves school they may have been a peer mediator for five or six years and have developed a range of skills that can be utilised in a community setting with the support of community youth workers.

RECRUITMENT AND SELECTION OF PEER MEDIATORS

A school's approach to recruitment and selection of mediators differs throughout Scotland. Some schools use application and/or nomination forms. This approach may be the fairest one; it allows pupils to self-select so the young people who apply are already interested in peer mediation. The application process gives a good indicator of relevant communication skills. Being nominated by a peer has the added benefit that a peer already thinks that the person nominated would make a good mediator.

It is important that the selection process operates on an equal opportunities basis. All pupils should be asked the same questions and there should be a consistent interviewer. It is also important to create a safe place to tell the pupil if they have been successful in the interview or not. Feedback should be given to all the pupils who participated in the interview process. It is crucial to remember that mediators need to practice regularly; realistically there is unlikely to be enough mediation work to occupy a very large number of mediators.

Some schools train a whole year group or class group and then do a further selection from the participants. This approach is often used where the school has identified one particular year group where there are recurring issues around conflict and bullying. Some peer mediation trainers suggest that the opportunity to work creatively within a specific year group adds value by giving all the children additional life skills. Choosing to train just a whole year group produces the problem of sustainability of the service because these children will mostly leave school together which could end the service. Another approach is to train a whole year group then ask them to self select. This has the added advantage of ensuring mediators feel confident to do the job but has some obvious disadvantages!

Some schools "up-skill" their buddies or members of the pupil council. Often the school will make the decision about the recruitment and selection process in consultation with the peer mediation trainer. Selecting pupils who already have completed additional skills training — like buddy training — works to build on the skills of pupils who have already undergone some kind of interpersonal skills training. One advantage is that the school already has a group of pupils trained in some basic mediation skills, such as active listening and communicating clearly. One disadvantage is that investment appears to be made in training the same set of pupils all the time. This can sometimes cause the school difficulties as it may upset some children and parents.

Selecting individuals for mediation training by teaching staff works where the staff are able to identify pupils who would benefit from the training and who already demonstrate the necessary skills to become a mediator. It is widely accepted that it is essential to select pupils from a wide variety of ability. A peer mediation team is more likely to be effective when individuals have a range of experiences and skills and where the selected team includes some pupils who have "street credibility".

SUSTAINABILITY

The sustainability of peer mediation can be an issue in some schools. There are a number of factors to take into account:

- Who in the staff team will take the lead role in supporting peer mediation?
- Where will peer mediation take place if the school has limited space?
- Who will support the peer mediators and provide ongoing training?
- Has the school adopted a "whole school" approach? If so, the service is more likely to be successful.

---

[4] Restorative Practices in Three Scottish Councils 2004–06: http://www.scotland.gov.uk/Publications/2007/08/23161140/0.

One of the ways to ensure the continuation of the service is to develop a group of trainers from the pool of trained peer mediators. This then enables the school to cascade peer mediation training throughout the school. In addition to staff involvement, the school may wish to include parents in the setting up and the training to help support peer mediation. If it is difficult to release staff to support peer mediation in the school it is possible to ask for parent volunteers. If the plan is to involve parents in this work it is important to complete the Disclosure Scotland process (criminal record check) and include them in any peer mediation training events.

Where the peer mediation service is available within a cluster of schools it may be that the secondary school in the cluster area has already trained peer mediators. This means that primary school peer mediators can feed into the secondary school's mediation team, and/or the secondary school peer mediators can help train in the primary schools. This is a good opportunity to bridge the transition from primary to secondary school. This also enables the schools to sustain the services from year to year.

RESTORATIVE PRACTICES PILOT PROGRAMME

The Scottish Government Education Department has a number of initiatives where peer mediation sits very comfortably. For example, the Curriculum for Excellence talks about successful learners, confident individuals, responsible citizens and effective contributors. In 2004, pilot projects for three local authority areas — North Lanarkshire, Highland, and Fife — were funded to support the development of innovative approaches as part of its commitment to promoting positive behaviour in Scottish schools.[4] Peer mediation was one of these approaches, as was restorative practices.

The main arena for restorative peer mediation in schools was in the playground, particularly in primary schools. In many instances some peer mediation/support initiatives were already being introduced when the pilots commenced. But these initiatives were expanded and further developed under the umbrella of restorative practices in ways which were often seen by senior management to have had a direct impact on school ethos and especially the culture of the playground.

Some schools, again more often the primary schools, felt that the aims of restorative practice and the aims of peer mediation were particularly compatible. In one authority (North Lanarkshire) the training materials developed by the authority for peer mediation were reviewed to provide a clear restorative basis and to introduce restorative language to senior primary pupils which they in turn would be able to use in their interactions with younger pupils.

In two primaries, where the development of peer mediation in playgrounds was new, senior staff reported "calmer" playtimes. The head teacher of one school talked of a noticeable positive impact on the understandings of pupils towards a restorative approach during the two years, and mentioned in particular the impact of positive peer pressure.

A number of schools had a system for logging playground incidents and in two primary schools the head teachers reported that both the rate and the severity of the incidents decreased over the 2-year period of the pilot project. It was also noted that there were fewer calls on the first aid box and also that post-break discipline referrals had decreased.

When asked about their role as peer mediators, "problem solvers", "playground pals" or "buddies", one P7 pupil said, "We are not allowed to take sides, [we're] there to help to sort out their problems . . . we are just helping them sort it out."

Previous research has revealed that many pupils have an acute sense of the importance of fairness. "Not taking sides" was often seen as the most valuable feature of peer mediation among pupils. Most pupils interviewed for the pilot project valued the role played by peer mediators. In some Highland and North Lanarkshire primary schools, mediation is led only by the oldest pupils. In Fife primary schools, there are mediators around eight years old who support the youngest pupils and other mediators around 11 years old who supported the older pupils. This seemed to work well and pupils felt that the mediators were able to make appropriate decisions about whether or not a problem needs to be handed on to an adult.

Of course, sometimes mediators need and want to play, so it is important to have a balance between responsibility and fun. A reservation was expressed by some P7 pupils in Benvane Primary who had concerns about their peers helping them sort out problems. Their reservations draw attention to the way in which the term "peer" is often used in this context. In schools, it does not usually refer to pupils of the same age. It might be argued that it is a misnomer because it is usually a much older pupil offering support to a younger one.

In secondary schools, the introduction of mediation or peer support was generally at an earlier stage than in the primary schools. S6 pupils interviewed in Marsco Secondary, for example, spoke very positively about being mediators for S1. They felt that they had a valuable role to play in supporting younger pupils and providing a bridge between them and teachers. However, the extent to which restorative practice had altered approaches to buddying or mediation is not as clear as in some of the primary schools. These senior pupils did not talk about a "process" or about using restorative language. However, it may be that as peer mediation continues to develop in secondary schools these questions can be considered more fully.

IS YOUR SCHOOL READY FOR PEER MEDIATION?

There are a number of important issues for schools to consider before setting up a peer mediation service.

- What are the goals for this project and why now?
- Who will deliver the training? If the staff have been trained then they may wish to deliver the training themselves. Alternatively, the whole staff team may wish to be trained by an external trainer.
- How does it fit with the School Development Plans?
- Is this a whole school initiative?
- Who will support the service?
- What time, training, funding, and resources will be required?
- What year groups will be involved?
- How many children will be involved?
- How will pupils be selected for the training?

How involved will parents be? Involving parents in the initial set up of peer mediation can help with the ongoing service provision and can tackle the issue of sustainability.

Once a school has considered the answer to these questions, then it is time to contact a peer mediation trainer.

OPTIONS FOR PEER MEDIATION IN SCOTLAND

Acknowledging the growth and development of peer mediation in Scotland, the Scottish Mediation Network has developed practice standards for peer mediation in Scotland. These standards include guidelines for practice support for peer mediators. Peer mediators are encouraged to become part of the mediation community and can join the Scottish Mediation Network free of charge. Work is in progress to have a number of continuing professional development training packs available on the SMN website to ensure teachers have easy access to materials so that peer mediators have on-going training after their initial peer mediation training. Topics such as "Active Listening", "Triangle Talks" (a system for peer support) "Managing Conflict", and "What is Bullying?" will be covered. Having free resources available is intended to benefit the peer mediation community in Scotland and should go some way to tackle the issue of sustainability.

This move towards improving standards and developing a system of ongoing training and support should make it possible for schools and peer mediators to join the Scottish Mediation Register. Our vision is to have peer mediation and conflict resolution as part of the curriculum in all schools as a way of embedding mediation into the culture in Scotland.

Peer mediation in schools in Scotland is increasing year on year. It is estimated that, as of 2008, around 120 schools in Scotland have a peer mediation service. The way peer mediation has developed varies from one local authority area to another and depends largely on three elements: how the programme is funded; the reason for implementing a peer mediation service; and the plans for its sustainability.

There is no doubt in my mind from the work I do in schools and the many adults, children and young people I speak with that peer mediation creates a change in playground culture and a shift in the behaviour of children involved in the training. To quote my favourite story, when I asked a wee boy what he thought of peer mediation, he told me that peer mediation was rubbish. When I asked him why he thought this, his reply was "Naebody fights anymore".

Chapter 14

ADDITIONAL SUPPORT NEEDS MEDIATION

Morag Steven

Additional Support Needs (ASN) mediation is a relatively new and developing field in Scotland and is the first kind of mediation to be included in legislation of the Scottish Parliament.

The Education (Additional Support for Learning) (Scotland) Act 2004 (ASL Act) places duties on local authorities to provide access to independent mediation for disputes with parents and carers of children and young people with "additional support needs" when and if they arise. These new duties came into force on 14 November 2005. "The Act aims to ensure that all children and young people are provided with the necessary support to help them work towards achieving their fullest potential. It also promotes collaborative working among all those supporting children and young people."[1]

Other mechanisms are available for parents of children with additional support needs who are in disagreement with the school or education authority. These include independent external adjudication, education authority appeal committees, and the additional support needs tribunal. Unlike mediation, these other mechanisms are all forms of adjudication where parties submit their verbal or written evidence and an expert or panel of experts make a decision. Similar to court proceedings, one side wins and the other loses.

Understandably there has been some confusion among parents and also educationalists about which method of dispute resolution is most suitable for different issues, and it is recognised that there is still much work to do in order to raise awareness about independent mediation and its potential benefits.

---

[1] "Supporting Children's Learning: Code of Practice", Statutory Guidance relating to the Education (Additional Support for Learning) (Scotland) Act (Scottish Executive, 2005).

WHAT ARE ADDITIONAL SUPPORT NEEDS?

The law says that children or young people may have additional support needs if they are unable to benefit from their school education without help beyond what is normally given to children or young people of the same age. Some examples of issues that could result in a child needing extra help include:

- social or emotional difficulties;
- behavioural difficulties;
- problems at home;
- bullying;
- being particularly gifted;
- a sensory impairment or communication problem;
- a physical disability;
- being a young carer or parent;
- moving frequently;
- having English as an additional language.

It is not possible to list all the circumstances that may mean a child needs additional support because every child is different. Children may need additional support at any stage during their time at school, and for differing lengths of time. For more information, a useful publication is "The Parents' Guide to Additional Support for Learning" available from Enquire.[2]

CASE STUDY 1

Mrs Brown had been trying to get help for her son Stuart for a number of months, with little success. Stuart is five, very withdrawn, does not interact well with other children or adults he does not know well, and needs routine. Stuart will soon make the move from nursery to primary school and Mrs Brown is getting increasingly worried about how he will cope with all the change.

The education authority told Mrs Brown that as Stuart met all his developmental targets, he did not have additional support needs so did not need any help. She was angry and upset about this and felt that no one at the authority was listening to her. Mrs Brown decided to look at other primary schools and found one offering the specific

---

[2] "The Parents' Guide to Additional Support for Learning" (Enquire: http://www. enquire.org.uk/pcp/pub/pcpguides.php).

support that she felt would benefit Stuart. She decided to make a placing request. The education authority refused her placing request because it felt Stuart did not have additional support needs and provision at his local school would be suitable. Mrs Brown wanted to appeal the refusal but decided to try mediation first. She contacted the education authority to inform them of her decision so it could begin the process.

The independent mediation service got in touch with Mrs Brown and the contact person at the education authority. Mrs Brown met the independent mediator to share information about her concerns and learn more about mediation. The same opportunity was given to the education officer involved. Both parties then met at the local voluntary centre, with the mediator there to facilitate their discussions.

Mrs Brown expressed how she felt about the handling of her son's education and how concerned she was about her belief that his needs were not even recognised. The education officer referred to a report from the educational psychologist which said that Stuart did indeed have some additional support needs, but that these could be met within the school nominated by the education authority for Stuart to attend. Mrs Brown and the education officer had the opportunity to negotiate the best way forward for Stuart.

Mrs Brown is happier that Stuart's needs are recognised and that her concerns have been listened to. She will still consider whether to appeal against the refusal of the placing request.[3]

CASE STUDY 2

Gordon is 14 and has been diagnosed with dyslexia and attention deficit hyperactivity disorder. He has been excluded a considerable number of times over the years for bad behaviour at school. Recently he was involved in a serious incident at school and was excluded again, but this time senior management at the school questioned whether he should be allowed to return at all. Some people involved, including the educational psychologist, thought that Gordon could do better at a different school.

The education authority called a meeting but it became clear that people were becoming more and more entrenched in their views. Mrs Nairn, Gordon's mother, was very clear that she wanted Gordon to return to school as soon as possible and didn't want him

---

[3] Case study used with permission from "The Parents' Guide to Additional Support for Learning" (Enquire: http://www.enquire.org.uk/pcp/publications/php), p 81.

to be transferred to another school. The meeting became quite heated.

The education authority contacted the independent mediation service and asked them to get involved. Mrs Nairn was also contacted and the mediator spent some time both with her and Gordon explaining about mediation and hearing their stories. At the mediation meeting (which Gordon chose not to attend), everyone involved spent some time considering all the available options to resolve the problem.

Everyone agreed that the educational environment of a large secondary school was making Gordon's difficulties worse. Eventually a solution was reached that everyone felt was fair and reasonable. Gordon would remain at home and out of school, but the education authority would provide a teaching package with home-visiting teachers. When the situation was reviewed by mutual agreement after three months everyone, including Gordon, was very pleased with the arrangements and the progress Gordon had made. Everyone agreed that it was not appropriate for him to return to school yet, but they would have regular reviews to consider the situation further.

THE ASN MEDIATION PROCESS

Because there are a variety of ASN mediation service providers in Scotland, it is impossible to state exactly how an ASN mediation session would be delivered. ASN mediation aims to be flexible and meet the needs of the people involved. However, it would be reasonable to expect the following steps.

First, the mediator contacts everyone involved individually to talk things through in private. These first meetings are important to help the various parties work out what key issues they want to discuss at mediation. Meetings with parents and their child usually take place in the home. Depending on the complexity of the case there can be a number of different parties involved such as class teacher, classroom auxiliary, head teacher, education officer, educational psychologist, therapist, social worker, as well as the child or young person and her/his parents or carers. Meetings with these people normally take place at their place of work. This first step of identifying the appropriate people to come to the mediation meeting and exploring their issues and concerns can sometimes be fairly time-consuming. However it is very important that everyone is well prepared for the mediation meeting.

Once everyone is ready, the mediator will arrange a joint meeting for everyone to talk openly and honestly about the situation, and look for solutions. These joint mediation sessions always take place in a neutral private venue that is suitable for all the parties. These meetings normally take up to two hours but if people need more time, that can be arranged with everyone's agreement. Occasionally more than one meeting is required in order to discuss fully all the issues. In situations where there are a considerable number of people in the room, two mediators will work together to facilitate the discussion.

During the mediation meeting the mediator will make sure that everyone gets an opportunity to talk, listen, express their concerns and explore what options may be available. The mediator helps keep everyone focussed on the discussion, summarises what has been said and helps everyone to move towards a solution that is manageable and sustainable. Whatever the outcome, a written account is given to all involved after the joint meeting. This is not a legally binding document.

Even if an agreement has not been reached, parties involved in additional support needs mediation can leave with an enhanced perspective of the issues and a greater understanding of other people's points of view. Other options for resolving the dispute may still be available.

Issues suitable for ASN mediation include:

- difficult or poor communication;
- broken relationships between parents and staff;
- school placement;
- level of support for a child with additional support needs;
- exclusion from school;
- transition of a record of needs to a co-ordinated support plan;
- non-attendance at school;
- transport issues.

This list is not comprehensive; many more issues can be dealt with successfully by using ASN mediation. The common theme in many ASN mediation cases is a desire to improve or restore communication between parents of a child with additional support needs and the school.

INVOLVING THE CHILD OR YOUNG PERSON IN MEDIATION

At the centre of the types of disputes discussed here is a child or young person with additional support needs who may be experiencing difficulties at school. However, it is the adults involved in supporting the child, whether at home or in school, who tend to be the key players in any dispute, often taking up entrenched positions. ASN mediation aims to maintain the focus on the needs of the child or young person, and the mediator will encourage the child to have her/his views included in the mediation process. The Standards in Scotland's Schools etc Act 2000 states that an education authority must have due regard to the views of children and young people in decisions that affect their education.[4]

ASN mediators will make every effort to meet with the child to hear his views, but their involvement in the mediation process will depend on a number of factors. Depending on the nature of the additional support needs, the mediator may have to use different methods to obtain their views such as videos, taped messages or drawings. Working with a child who, for example, is visually impaired with significant learning disabilities and speech and language difficulties can prove challenging for a mediator who has no prior knowledge of these types of difficulties. In situations like this, advice will be sought from the child's parents or people who know him well about the best way to communicate in a meaningful way for the child. Sometimes an advocate, befriender or other support worker can help the child express their views.

It is not always appropriate to have the child or young person present at the joint mediation meetings, particularly if emotions are running high. Because mediation is a flexible process, there is no hard and fast rule about this. Sometimes children and young people attend the meeting for part of the time and then leave. Sometimes an advocate or supporter can present the child's views to the meeting in his or her absence.

FEEDBACK FROM ASN MEDIATION SERVICE USERS

(Collated from users of Common Ground Mediation and Resolve: ASL)

Question: *What was the most useful thing about mediation?*

Answer: "An independent person's views and impartiality. It was a positive experience." (Head Teacher)

Question: *Did you get what you expected from mediation?*

Answer: "Yes. I am confident that both parties came away from the mediation with a clearer idea of the issues and a positive way forward." (Education Manager)

Question: *What worked well during the mediation?*

Answer: "Getting the chance to make sure everyone understood what was being said and agreed to. Independence from

---

[4] Standards in Scotland's Schools etc Act 2000 (Scottish Executive, June 2000): http:// www.opsi.gov.uk/legislation/scotland/acts2000/asp_20000006_en 1.

the education system allowed for a less intimidating discussion." (Parent)

HISTORY OF ASN MEDIATION IN SCOTLAND

In the period before the 2004 Act was introduced, the Scottish Executive funded a number of voluntary organisations to develop mediation in the field "Special Educational Needs (SEN) mediation". The new term "additional support needs" was introduced with the ASL Act.

Enquire, the Scottish advice service for additional support for learning, received funding from 1999 to 2004, and set up the first mediation pilot, providing free mediation services to five local authorities: South Lanarkshire, Stirling, East Dunbartonshire, Argyll and Bute and Glasgow City. Volunteer mediators were recruited and trained in 2001, and a further group of more experienced mediators joined in 2002. Funding for Enquire's mediation service came to an end in March 2004. However, Children in Scotland, the voluntary organisation that manages Enquire, then set up a new ASN mediation service called Resolve: ASL.

In Highland, CHESS (Children in the Highlands Education Support Service) and in Perth and Kinross, Angus and Dundee City, Parent-to-Parent were funded to develop SEN mediation until March 2004.

The Govan Law Centre's Education Law Unit also received funding to develop SEN mediation in parts of Scotland where it had not been previously trialled. Respect Mediation, as part of the Govan Law Centre, undertook a consultation exercise on SEN mediation, and a report was also produced in 2004, as a guide to setting up and delivering mediation services in the Scottish education system.[5]

The report included a number of recommendations:

1. Serious consideration should be given to the development of a national ASN mediation service, in order to establish uniform standards of mediation across the country.

2. A national, centrally funded ASN mediation service is likely to be the most cost efficient model.

3. Every ASN mediation service must be fully independent of education authorities so that users of the service can have full confidence in its neutrality.

4. The Govan Law Centre Code of ASN Mediation Practice should be adopted as a national minimum standard for ASN mediation services.

---

[5] Available online at:www.edlaw.org.uk/ASNMed.pdf.

5. Further consideration should be given to the appropriate stage in disputes for referral to independent mediation.

6. The principle of voluntary participation is crucial to mediation, and pressure must not be exerted on parties to participate.

7. Consideration needs to be given to ensure the views of the child/young person with additional support needs are included in the mediation process.

8. Methods of monitoring and evaluating ASN mediation need to be put in place in order to measure standards of work against "best practice".

9. Information about the availability of independent ASN mediation should be freely available, for example, in school handbooks and education department publications.

10. Consideration should be given to the potential benefits of the use of mediation as a method of dispute resolution not only in the area of additional support needs, but in all aspects of education provision.

Current ASN mediation provision in Scotland has developed using most of these recommendations.

ASN MEDIATION IN 2008

Resolve: ASL (managed by Children in Scotland) and Common Ground Mediation are the two main providers of ASN mediation in Scotland, and between them have service level agreements with 20 out of the 32 local authorities. Some local authorities have contracts with other mediation services, some local authorities have an "in-house" mediation service, and a small number of local authorities appear to have no provision at all, despite it being a legal duty. The result is somewhat of a patchwork of ASN mediation provision.

However, for the last few years an ASN Mediation Initiative Group has been operating under the auspice of the Scottish Mediation Network. The aims of this group include: sharing information about the development of ASN mediation in different local authority areas; exploring areas of common interest for service providers; and developing good practice guidelines and national standards. Scottish Quality Standards for ASN Mediation service providers have been developed and are available at

www.commongroundmediation.co.uk.

The Scottish Mediation Register is another useful resource.

In October 2007, Her Majesty's Inspectorate of Education (HMIE) published its report on the implementation of the Education (Additional Support for Learning) (Scotland) Act 2004.[6] It concluded that services for mediation and dispute resolution were effective: "In around a quarter of authorities where parents had used mediation services, both parents and key staff felt that intervention had been effective and helpful in resolving the dispute." However, the report acknowledges that there is still work to do regarding raising awareness of mediation and its potential benefits: "In around a quarter of authorities, school-based staff expressed concern about whether parents were sufficiently aware of procedures for resolving disagreements."

CONTACTING AN ASN MEDIATOR

By law, local education authorities must provide mediation services free of charge for parents, carers and young people. Parents of children with additional support needs should contact the ASL information officer in their local authority. If they do not know who this person is, they can contact Enquire to find out, on 0845 123 2303. Or they can telephone the local council and ask to be put through to the relevant person. Alternatively, the Scottish Mediation Network can advise which independent mediation service provider operates in particular areas of Scotland. Schools and education authorities can also contact their local mediation service provider to start the mediation process.

---

[6] Available online at: http://www.hmie.gov.uk/Publications.aspx.

CODE OF PRACTICE FOR MEDIATION IN SCOTLAND

Preamble

This Code is intended to form a baseline for the conduct of all forms of mediation in Scotland. It is expected that the different strands of mediation will, if they have not already done so, develop complementary and more detailed guidance.

Mediation

Mediation is a process in which disputing parties seek to build agreement and/or improve understanding with the assistance of a trained mediator acting as an impartial third party. Mediation is voluntary and aims to offer the disputing parties the opportunity to be fully heard, to hear each other's perspectives and to decide how to resolve their dispute themselves.

Voluntary participation and self determination

A mediator shall recognise that mediation is based on the principle of voluntary participation and that it is the parties, rather than the mediator, who determine the outcome.

Impartiality and independence

A mediator shall remain impartial and independent. If a mediator becomes aware of any reason which may diminish their impartiality or independence, they shall disclose this to the parties at the earliest opportunity and withdraw from the mediation unless the parties do not wish them to do so.

Conflicts of interest

A mediator shall disclose all actual and potential conflicts of interest reasonably known to the mediator whether before or during a mediation and shall withdraw from the mediation unless the parties do not wish him/her to do so.

Competence

A mediator shall be responsible for undertaking sufficient training, supervision and continuing professional development to maintain necessary mediation skills. A mediator shall mediate only when she/he believes that she/he has the necessary skills to carry out the mediation.

Confidentiality

Confidentiality in mediation is important to encourage all participants to speak truthfully and candidly, and to enable a full exploration of issues in dispute. Unless compelled by law, or with the consent of all the parties, a mediator shall not disclose any of the information given during the mediation process.

Understanding of mediation

A mediator shall ensure that the parties understand:

- the purpose and procedure of the mediation;
- the role of the parties and the mediator;
- any fee arrangement;
- the obligation of confidentiality.

Advertising and solicitation

In advertising or offering services, mediators shall not guarantee settlement or promise specific results. All information provided by mediators about their education, background, mediation training and experience shall be accurate.

Gifts and favours

A mediator must not accept from or exchange any gift or favour with any party in any mediation. A mediator must use judgement that reflects the high ethical standards which mediation requires.

Discrimination

People should always be treated with respect and without discrimination.

Complaints and professional indemnity insurance

A mediator shall provide information about the process for handling any complaint made about their conduct or service, and about any professional indemnity insurance cover they may have.

Appendix 2

RESOURCES

Further reference addresses for the mediation sectors and organisations detailed in the chapters are below. These are correct as at December 2008.

To find a mediator or mediation service:

Go to the Scottish Mediation Register:
www.scottishmediationregister.org.uk and

the map of mediation in Scotland:
www.scottishmediation.org.uk/mediators/index.asp

For information on the work of the Scottish Mediation Network:

Scottish Mediation Network
18 York Place
Edinburgh
EH1 3EP
(0131) 556 1221
www.scottishmediation.org.uk

For information on community mediation:

Scottish Community Mediation Centre
21 Abercromby Place
Edinburgh
EH3 6QE
(0131) 624 9200
www.scmc.sacro.org.uk

For information on family mediation:

Relationships Scotland
18 York Place
Edinburgh
EH1 3EP
0845 119 2020
www.relationships-scotland.org.uk

and

CALM, the association of family law mediators accredited by the Law Society of Scotland:
www.calmscotland.co.uk

For information on sheriff court referred mediation:

Edinburgh Sheriff Court Mediation Service
27 Chambers Street
Edinburgh
EH1 1LB
(0131) 220 1092

For information on rights-based conciliation:

Disability Conciliation Service
Mediation Works
16 Queen Street
Wellington
Shropshire
TF1 IEH
(01952) 224285
www.dcs-gb.com

Equality and Human Rights Commission Helpline Scotland
Freepost RRLL-GYLB-UJTA
The Optima Building
58 Robertson Street
Glasgow
G2 8DU
0845 604 5510 – Scotland Main
0845 604 5520 – Scotland Textphone
www.equalityhumanrights.com

INDEX